Garden of the Soul

Garden of the Soul

Exploring Metaphorical Landscapes of Spirituality

MARK MAH

WIPF & STOCK · Eugene, Oregon

GARDEN OF THE SOUL
Exploring Metaphorical Landscapes of Spirituality

Copyright © 2014 Mark Mah. All rights reserved. Except for brief quotations in critical publications or reviews, no part of this book may be reproduced in any manner without prior written permission from the publisher. Write: Permissions, Wipf and Stock Publishers, 199 W. 8th Ave., Suite 3, Eugene, OR 97401.

All Scripture quotations, unless otherwise noted, are from The Holy Bible, New International Version®, NIV® Copyright © 1973, 1978, 1984, 2011 by Biblica, Inc.™ Used by permission. All rights reserved worldwide.

Wipf & Stock
An imprint of Wipf and Stock Publishers
199 W. 8th Ave., Suite 3
Eugene, OR 97401

www.wipfandstock.com

isbn 13: 9978-1-62564-401-5

Manufactured in the U.S.A.

In memory of

my mother and brother

Contents

1 The Power of Metaphor | 1
2 Garden of Growth | 18
3 River of Life | 37
4 Sea of Turbulence | 53
5 Desert of Transformation | 70
6 Mountain of Challenge | 89

Conclusion | 106

Bibliography | 111

1

The Power of Metaphor

> Strange words simply puzzle us; ordinary words convey only what we know already. It is from metaphor that we can best get hold of something fresh.
>
> —Aristotle[1]

TELL IT SLANT

WHAT IS THE BEST approach for a prophet to rebuke a powerful king about his misdemeanor without losing his life? If the prophet confronts the king directly he may turn defensive and deny his wrongdoing. How can the prophet go about telling the king of his wrongdoing, getting him to admit his sins, and at the same time saving his own life? The way is to take an indirect approach or to "tell it slant."

The prophet Nathan, instead of directly confronting King David of his sins of adultery and murder, decided to "tell it slant"

---

1. Aristotle, *The Rhetoric and Poetics of Aristotle*, 186.

by the use of a metaphorical story. He told the king that a certain town has two inhabitants: a rich man who owns a large number of sheep and cattle and a poor man who has nothing except one little ewe lamb. The poor man treats the lamb like his own child. It shares his food, drinks from his cup, and sleeps in his lap. Apparently the little lamb is the poor man's most precious asset. Now a guest comes to the rich man's house. Instead of killing one of his livestock to prepare a meal for his guest, he decides to slaughter the poor man's ewe lamb to serve his guest (2 Sam 12:1–7).

David, on hearing this story, was furious and angry at the rich man. The king declared that the man deserved to die because he showed no pity on the poor and helpless. He should pay four times the price of the ewe lamb as compensation for mistreating the poor man. David was fuming because he abhorred the injustice meted out by the rich man in this story. It was not right to take someone else's property when one could afford not to. It was unjust to take advantage of someone who neither had the power nor means to resist. It was immoral to deprive someone his only valuable asset that gave him the most joy.

David's behavior and reaction to the story is expected. He is expected to stand up for the poor and oppressed in society as Israel's king. As judge he defends the afflicted and saves the needy from the oppressor. Under the monarchy in Israel, the king is the final court of appeal because he is responsible for the promotion of justice and righteousness in the land. It is a common practice for people to bring their complaints to the king seeking justice. An example is the case of the woman from Tekoa who appeals to King David to intervene on behalf of her son in order to save him from those who want his life (2 Sam 14:4–11). Another classic example is the famous story of two women who seek King Solomon's help to settle a dispute over who is the real mother of a newborn baby (1 Kgs 3:6–28).

Nathan seized the opportunity to reveal who the rich man was. He pointed his finger at the king and said, "You are the man." In the story told by the prophet, David was the rich man, the poor man was Uriah the Hittite, and the ewe lamb was Bathsheba.

The Power of Metaphor

Earlier David had an affair with Uriah's wife and got her pregnant. David schemed to have Uriah killed in battle in order to cover up his sin. He used his power to cover up his sins thinking that no one would know. Nathan was able to convince the king of his criminal behavior by using metaphors to tell a familiar story. He was able to save his neck as well by "telling it slant."

A metaphor makes use of visual language to grab attention and invoke the emotions of the listener. Even the phrase "I *see* what you mean" is metaphorical. It figuratively means, "I understand what you are saying." David did not use his eyes to listen to the prophet Nathan. He got the message loud and clear by listening to the story. He was enlightened when he identified himself with the story at the emotional and cognitive level.

We tend to respond more easily and intuitively to images than just explanatory words. The caption "Smoking is bad for health" is printed on every box of cigarettes sold in the market. The caption is obviously not working as expected. Graphic pictures of cancerous tumors and diseased lungs are now printed on every cigarette box. Recently, the Australian government went a step further by having every box printed in a certain shade of dull green. Hopefully, along with the graphic pictures, this will deter more people from taking up the habit of smoking. This morning, while driving home after a good workout of climbing and walking at the botanical gardens, I came across an accident. A smashed-up motorbike was left by the roadside. The sight really shocked me when I noticed the dried blood stains on the road. At that moment, I cautioned myself to be more careful on the road. I would not have this kind of resolve if I just read about the accident in a newspaper.

A good metaphor appeals to the senses, especially the sense of sight. In this case a picture is worth more than a thousand words. A picture of a steaming cup of coffee or soup invokes the feeling of warmth and homeliness to many people. It reminds them of the warmth and comfort of home. At one time, the makers of Campbell Soup decided to redesign its packaging. Responding to customers' comments, the company added steam rising above pictures of soup of tomato, mushroom or chicken. Previously pictures

3

of soup were without steam. Customers indicated that they were emotionally connected to the product if it looked warm.²

THINKING METAPHORICALLY

The pervasive use of metaphors in all sectors of our life is highlighted by James Geary. In his book *I Is An Other*, he writes:

> Metaphor conditions our interpretations of the stock market and, through advertising, it surreptitiously infiltrates our purchasing decisions. In the mouths of politicians, metaphor subtly nudges public opinion; in the minds of business people, it spurs creativity and innovation. In science, metaphor is the preferred nomenclature for new theories and new discoveries; in psychology, it is the natural language of human relationships and emotions.³

Take for instance a weather report broadcasted in Australia (italics are metaphors):

> Perth is *in the grip* of a heat wave with temperatures set to soar to 40 degrees Celsius by the end of the week. Australia is *no stranger* to extreme weather. Melbourne was pummeled with *hailstones the size of golf balls* on Saturday. Long term, droughts, bushfires, and floods have all *plagued* swathes of Queensland, New South Wales and Victoria."⁴

Five metaphors are used in this short paragraph. One metaphor is used for every eleven words. The severity of the weather is highlighted by describing hailstones as big as golf balls and extreme weather conditions to that of a biblical plague. We like to use metaphors to describe the weather in ordinary conversation: "It rained cats and dogs last night," or "The wind howled throughout the night."

2. Greary, *I Is An Other*, 84.
3. Ibid., 3.
4. Ibid., 5.

The Power of Metaphor

Politicians love to communicate using metaphors. People identify easily with metaphors because they are familiar and easy to understand. Metaphors make complex ideas simple because they compare an abstract or unknown concept to what the listener already knows. Take for example, the term "fiscal cliff," coined by Ben Bernanke, chairman of the United States Federal Reserve. According to some economists, the danger of falling over the "fiscal cliff" would have become a reality if expiring tax cuts and overall government spending cuts were not resolved by the end of 2012. The country would have plunge into a recession if these two measures were allowed to proceed as scheduled. This would have undermined consumer confidence, depressed household incomes, increased unemployment rates, and weakened the stock market. The mental image of falling over the cliff made people uneasy and insecure. The government was hard pressed by the public to do something about the "fiscal cliff" before the deadline was reached.

When Deng Xiaoping, the paramount leader who ruled China from 1978 to 1989, was asked about the imminent rise of corruption due to China opening her doors to a market economy, he replied with these words: "When you open the door, flies will get in." In other words, it is inevitable that corruption will take place, but the benefits of a market economy far outweigh the negative effects of corrupted practices. Deng was not sure where the country was moving economically when she opened her doors to the world. When asked for a roadmap he had none because the country was still experimenting and getting used to an economy set by the market and not by planners. He replied using these words: "Cross the river by feeling the stones with your feet."

Our brain is wired to think metaphorically because it has the capacity for imagination. We find difficulty in communicating and making sense of the world without the use of metaphors. Metaphors are so pervasive in our daily living that we are often unaware of them even when we use them all the time. As mentioned, the metaphorical phrase, "I see what you mean" is used so often that we do not think of it as a metaphor anymore. Statements like "Time flies" or "It's a jungle out there" have become part of our everyday conversation.

Tony Blair, former prime minister of the United Kingdom, gave a speech on school reforms in 2005:

> Over the last fifty years, state education has improved. And that improvement has *accelerated* in the last eight years. But successive reforms since the war have not always *delivered* all that they aimed to *deliver*. What is different this time is that we have learned what works. We have the experience of successful schools. What we must see now is a system of independent state schools, underpinned by fair admissions and fair funding, where parents are equipped and enabled to *drive* improvement, *driven* by the aspiration of parents (our italics).[5]

Most of us are not aware that the metaphors used in this speech aim to reflect a worldview with the intent to shape thinking and influence public opinions on education. The words in italics *(accelerated, deliver, driven)* are mechanistic metaphors used to imply that education can be engineered mechanically like a well-oiled machine.[6] The state government, the school, and parents must play their assigned roles to foster greater growth and efficiency. The government's role is to draft policies that promote fair play and funding. The parents, who harbor high hopes for their children to excel educationally, will assume the role of motivator to apply pressure on the schools to perform. The schools, given the independence and mandate to chart their own course and set fair standards, should be able to deliver the results. If each party, like different parts of a machine, fulfills its assigned roles or functions, the expected outcome is inevitable.

POWER TO INFLUENCE

The power of metaphors to influence minds and shape public opinions was authenticated by researchers Paul Thibodeau and

---

5. Quoted in Lumby and English, *Leadership as Lunacy*, 4.
6. Ibid., 5.

The Power of Metaphor

Lera Boroditsky from Stanford University.[7] In this experiment, the researchers asked 482 students to read one of two reports about crime in the city of Addison. After reading the reports they were told to suggest solutions to tackle the crime problem in Addison. In the first report, crime was described as a "wild beast preying on the city" and "lurking in the neighborhoods." After reading the first report, 75 percent of the students opted for a tougher solution of enforcement and punishment, such as having more jails and calling for the military to help address the problem. Only 25 percent of the students advocated social reforms like better health care, improved education, or reviving the economy.

The second report was exactly the same as the first except crime was now described as a "virus infecting the city" and "plaguing" the city. After reading the second report, the percentage of students opting for a tougher solution dropped to 56 percent and those advocating social reforms jumped to 44 percent. Surprisingly, the majority of the students identified the crime statistics in the report, and not the language, that had influenced their decisions. Only 3 percent of the students were observant enough to identify the differing crime metaphors as having an influence on their decision making.

Chrysler, the company that made cars, was in financial trouble in 1980. It needed a loan of $1.2 billion from the United States government to bail it out. Congress at that time was cool to the idea of using citizen's money to bail out the company. The company's CEO, Lee Iacocca, had to find a way to convince the government that it was in its interest to approve the mega-loan. He used a clever metaphor in order to change Congress's perception. He used the image of a "safety net" instead of "bail out." To bail out gives the perception of throwing money into a hole. A safety net is different. It is a preventive act to avoid danger or collapse. He argued convincingly that all governments were in the business of providing safety nets for her citizens. Chrysler was no exception because the company had a large workforce whose members were also citizens of the United States. No one in the government

---

7. Gorlick, "Is Crime a Virus or Beast?"

wanted to deny a hardworking employee a safety net. The earlier resistance of Congress changed because of this new perception. Congress came to see the social benefits of the loan to help the car company tide over bad times. Lee Iacocca got the money he asked with this metaphor.[8]

Psychologists love to experiment using metaphors to prime the behavior of unsuspecting students. In one experiment, students were asked to form sentences using various sets of words. One group was given words that carried an elderly theme though the word "old" was never used. Words like "bald," "forgetful," "walking stick," "gray," or "wrinkle" were scrambled with other neutral words. The control group was given words with no particular characteristics. When they finished making the sentences, students were told to walk from one point to the next. The time to complete the distance was measured. As predicted, the group of students that made sentences using words with an elderly theme walked significantly slower than the control group. The set of words used by the students primed thoughts of old age though the word "old" was never mentioned. This thought again primed the behavior of students who walked slowly, which is associated with aging.[9]

METAPHORS IN SCRIPTURE

It was not surprising that people like Jesus, Paul, and many writers of Scripture are masters of metaphors since metaphors have the power to influence minds and shape opinions. Paul uses the metaphor of the human body to symbolize the church. He calls Jesus the "Bridegroom" and his church "the Bride of Christ." Jesus calls himself "the Way" and challenges many to follow him. He sees himself as "the Vine" and asks his followers to remain in him. He has compassion on the crowd for they are "like sheep without a shepherd." Jesus communicates truth by telling stories or parables. These stories are filled with metaphors that hearers

---

8. Miller, *Metaphorically Selling*, 1.
9. Kahneman, *Thinking, Fast and Slow*, 53.

The Power of Metaphor

can immediately understand because they are the stuff of everyday living. Jesus' stories speak of common objects that we see, touch, taste, hear, and smell every day. He talks about farmers and seed, rocks and paths, nets and fishermen, shepherds and sheep, stones and houses, bread and salt, pearls and pigs, figs and leaves, and many more. The people appreciate his stories because they appeal to the senses. They can relate to these stories not just cognitively but at the emotional level as well.

The difference between the Pharisees and Jesus is that Jesus loves to use metaphors to communicate to the common people. Parables are narrated metaphors. They are made-up stories placed in the context of the familiar and factual. The Pharisees, on the other hand, do not use language metaphorically. They don't tell stories. They want precision in their use of language. They like to use language to define, instruct, control, regulate, and defend. Their language lacks color, imagination, and excitement. The hearers immediately sense the difference in the teachings of Jesus and the Pharisees.[10] Unlike the teachers of the law, the hearers are amazed at his teaching because he teaches as one with authority (Matt 7:28–29).

Metaphors do more than just firing up the imagination. They require our participation and invite us to get involved. On hearing the stories we cannot just remain a bystander. Like David, we intuitively and emotionally take sides against the rich man for his selfishness in Nathan's story of the ewe lamb. Eugene Peterson, in his book *The Way of Jesus*, writes:

> Metaphor does that, makes me a participant in creating the meaning and entering into the action of the word. I can no longer understand the word by looking it up in the dictionary, for it is no longer just itself. It is alive and moving, inviting me to participate in the meaning. When the writers of Scripture use metaphor, we get involved with God.[11]

---

10. Peterson, *The Way of Jesus*, 214.
11. Ibid., 26.

Why do metaphors play such an important role in Scripture? Metaphors have the ability, not just to inform and persuade, but also to connect the known with the unknown, the visible with the invisible. Derived from the Greek roots *meta* (across, over) and *phor* (carry), it literally means "to carry over or across." It carries over or across something known and familiar to something unknown and unfamiliar. A metaphor takes a commonly used word that we know and experience and conveys meaning to something that cannot be verified by our senses. We experience the visible world around us through the use of our five senses. Through them we collect information, interpret, judge, and make decisions about our environment. We cannot do the same with the invisible world, though this world is just as real as the physical world around us. As Peterson explains, the quickest and easiest way to access the invisible world is by means of metaphorical language. It connects and makes indivisible the visible and invisible world because both worlds are the same world.[12]

Scripture records events that are rooted in the visible world. It locates the event in terms of people, place, and time. This is the "real" world because we are most familiar with it. Just as real is the spiritual world. It is an invisible world of angels, God, spiritual warfare, evil forces, and departed saints. In Scripture both worlds co-exist as one world. We are told to run the race on earth with perseverance because the past saints (cloud of witnesses) are there to cheer us on (Heb 12:1).

Once, a faithful Christian was paralyzed from the neck down due to a car accident. He sensed someone was in the hospital room while he was lamenting to God about his condition. He couldn't turn his head so he asked for a glass of water. There was no reply to his request. He knew, in his heart, that God was there with him in his pain even though he did not respond to his many prayers.

Prayer connects the visible world with the invisible. It is a bridge between earth and heaven and between the human and divine. It is inevitable that our prayer language is metaphorical when we use the things we experience in our visible world to depict who

12. Ibid., 25.

our God is. God's invisible qualities—his eternal power and divine nature—are made known through his creation. We address God as "Rock," "Shepherd," "Fortress," or "Mother." Metaphor is the bridge that links our sense experience with our faith experience. It uses the tangible to explain the invisible. Basil of Caesarea, one of the Cappadocian Fathers of the Eastern church, considers the created word as a school where we learn about God. Through the sight of visible and sensible things, "the mind is led by hand, to the contemplation of invisible things." He also tells us how this is done:

> I want creation to fill you with so much admiration that everywhere, wherever you may be, the least plant may bring to you the clear remembrance of the Creator. If you see grass, think of human nature, and remember the comparison of the wise Isaiah, "All flesh is grass, and all the goodliness thereof is as the flower of the field.[13]

My house is located behind a forested hill. From my kitchen window I can see huge boulders on the slope of the hill. It is difficult to remove these huge rocks for they look steady and strong. Moreover, these rocks have been there for a long time. These boulders are best to be left alone unless we have to remove them, using dynamite and at great cost. The psalmist has in mind a God who is powerful and able to deliver him from all his troubles when he addresses God as a rock.

> My God is my rock, in whom I take refuge. He is my shield and the horn of my salvation, my stronghold. I call to the Lord who is worthy of praise, and I am saved from my enemies. (Ps 18:2–3)

EXPLORING SPATIAL METAPHORS

This book aims to explore the use of metaphors in the area of spiritual formation. The reasons are many. Jesus and many writers of Scripture used metaphorical language to communicate effectively.

---

13. Basil of Caesarea, *Hexaemeron*, 8: 52, 76.

Garden of the Soul

It is easier to communicate and to make sense of the world around us with the use of metaphor because we are primed to think and feel metaphorically. Metaphor has a life of its own that is pervasive and influential. It carries its own voice that is not intimidating because it is non confrontational. It mediates truth that grabs our attention and provokes us to action. Metaphorical language can help us to access the invisible through the use of visible things that we know and experience. Significantly, metaphor has the ability to induce us to participate and get involved in matters of the soul. Parker Palmer writes:

> If soul truth is to be spoken and heard, it must be approached "on a slant" . . . But soul truth is so powerful that we must allow ourselves to approach it, and it to approach us, indirectly. We must invite, not command, the soul to speak. We must allow, not force, ourselves to listen.[14]

In this book we want to focus on spatial metaphors. Landscapes feature prominently in Scripture. Important, life-changing events often took place in specific locations in the Bible: Adam's first sin in the garden of Eden, John the Baptist baptizing in the Jordan River, Moses crossing the Red Sea, Jesus tempted in the desert and transfigured at Mount Tabor. The interrelationship between humans and landscape is attested in the Bible. Adam was formed out of the dust of the earth. He was named "Adam" because he was formed from the *adamah*, which is the Hebrew word for "ground." It is part of the divine order that humans are closely connected to the soil. Perhaps God called Adam to till the earth for this reason. The farmer stays close to the earth because his livelihood is dependent on it. We are all farmers, not in terms of occupation but by consumption.[15] We live by what farmers grow because our livelihood is dependent on what comes out from the ground. We see ourselves as part of an ecosystem where all organic life, including ours, is interrelated. We must not lose the sense of

---

14. Palmer, *A Hidden Wholeness*, 92.
15. Hiebert, "Eden: Moral Power of a Biblical Landscape," 16.

The Power of Metaphor

dependence demanded by our landscapes. It is understandable, from this perspective, for humans to attach or assign meaning and value to certain landscapes in their life.

POWER OF PLACE

What makes a place special? What gives a place its identity, its aura? Why certain places invoke a certain mood or feeling in us? I have good childhood memories of the place where I grew up. There was a small park just in front of the house where I grew up. I spent most of my free hours playing with neighborhood kids in this park, which is now occupied by a five-story building. The park was a perfect place for a child's playground. It was shady with many nooks and corners to play hide-and-seek. After school I would be in the park until it was time for dinner. The neighborhood has not changed though some development has taken place. I still have fond memories of the place. Each time I drive past the place I will slow down just to get a glimpse of the spot and try to recall the good times. The place has a special meaning for me because it gives me a warm feeling of openness, freedom, and friendship. My elementary school was a five-minutes walk from my home. Whenever I think of my elementary school, the jungle gym comes to my mind. I spent hours before and after school playing catch with friends and climbing up, down, and around the gym like little monkeys. I would momentarily look at the spot to see whether the gym was still there every time I passed by the school. The sight of it brought back fond memories of fun and freedom. One day, I felt a tinge of sadness because the spot was empty and the gym was no longer there anymore.

Physicists Niels Bohr and Werner Heisenberg once visited Kronberg Castle in Denmark. Bohr commented to Heisenberg that the castle took on a special meaning when they knew that Hamlet lived there. The thought of Hamlet having lived in that castle changed their feelings for the place: "Suddenly the walls and the ramparts speak a quite different language. The courtyard becomes an entire different world; a dark corner reminds us of the darkness in the human soul, we hear Hamlet's 'To be or not to be.'" Yet both scientists knew that Hamlet's real existence could not be proven, let alone that he lived at Kronberg Castle.[16]

If we attach meaning and value to a certain landscape then the setting can affect our behavior as well. In a formal setting we tend not to disturb the status quo. Certain places require us to behave in an appropriate manner. We find ourselves behaving differently when in a restaurant, library, museum, or subway. We find the liberty to talk in a restaurant but not in a library. Chinese restaurants are full of chatter. The talk gets louder when wine is served freely especially during wedding dinners. If we see others talking in a library we either gesture to signal for them to shut up or give them a stern stare indicating our disapproval. We tiptoe our way quietly in a museum but will not hesitate to rush ahead in order to get a vacant seat when taking the subway. The difference in behavior may be due to crowding in the subway whereas there is a lot of personal space inside a museum. People tend to be more aggressive, less helpful, and feel more depressed and withdrawn when taking the subway. These behavioral traits act as a psychological barrier to protect them from overstimulation in a crowded place.

One psychological shield is the home. Home is a special place for us because we know that we are in control of our own world the moment we step inside. We can do what we like in our own home that is not possible elsewhere. We are on our own turf that shields us from the grinding stress of working life, the noise of hurried, impatient traffic, and the glaring stare of strangers. It is here that we can enjoy our own privacy and intimacy. There is no place like home for many people. It is not unusual for some of us to bring along a photo or favorite toy from the home when we are away in a strange place. Research has shown that first-year students who decorate their dorm rooms with memorabilia from home or hometown are less likely to drop out of college than those who do not.[17]

16. Tuan, *Space and Place*, 4.
17. Gallagher, *The Power of Place*, 187–88.

The Power of Metaphor

LANDSCAPES OF SPIRITUAL FORMATION

We talk about an invisible world when we talk about spirituality. It is a world of faith, holiness, temptations, sin, perseverance, prayer, humility, hope, forgiveness, obedience, suffering, and love. This invisible world is not easy to grasp for many people. The use of metaphors will help to bring meaning and understanding to this invisible world of spirituality. Metaphorical landscapes are used in this book because they feature prominently in Scripture. Scripture attaches meaning and value to different biblical landscapes. Different landscapes project a different world and speak a different language that requires a different response.

A bountiful garden is food for the body and a delight to the eyes. The garden of Eden in Genesis is a fine example of such a place. The first couple was asked to tend the garden and to enjoy the fruits of their labor. They could have lived a utopian life of bliss if not for their disobedience to God. A garden needs water to keep it alive. In the book of Genesis, we are told that the garden of Eden was watered by four rivers running through it. In Revelation we are given a peep at paradise: a river of the water of life that runs from God's throne through the New Jerusalem, the Holy City of God. In heaven there will be no more sea because it speaks of turmoil and trials, separation and chaos. The disciples were struggling against the wind and waves that threatened to sink their fishing boat while they were trying hard to cross the Galilean Sea. The sea is filled with challenges. Jesus challenged the disciples to cast their net into the deep even after a night of futile fishing. He even challenged Peter to come to him walking on water.

The desert is as dry as the sea is wet. God led the nation of Israel in the desert wilderness for forty years. Jesus was led by the Holy Spirit to be tempted by Satan in the desert for forty days. The desert speaks of death and purification. Unlike the garden, nothing grows in the desert. Everything is magnified in the desert because of its purified air and harsh environment. The stars and moon seem larger and brighter. The sun is redder and bigger when it slowly sinks into the shimmering horizon like a bright ball of fire. The rhythmic sounds of insects and wild animals are sharper and more distinct in the desert than elsewhere. The desert trains us to pay close attention to the ordinary things of life. Deserts and mountains are fierce landscapes that test our nerves and resolve. The mountain plays a special role in Scripture. Moses met God and spoke to him face to face on Mount Sinai. Jesus was transfigured on top of a high mountain in the company of the three disciples. Elijah was battling with the Baal worshippers on Mount Carmel to determine which deity was more powerful. Moses was given the first glimpse of the Promised Land at Mount Nebo. Each had to take a journey to reach the top. It was at this vantage point that they were able to gain a better perspective of the divine power and presence. The mountain speaks of catching a vision of God just like Moses catching a vision of the Promised Land. The knowledge and presence of God are so intense and direct that we are fully present to God as he is fully present to us.

I have chosen these five biblical landscape metaphors to aid us in the journey of spiritual formation. It is hoped that these spatial metaphors of garden, river, sea, desert, and mountain will help us not only to understand but will make us want to participate and get involved in nurturing our spiritual life. These metaphors, with their vivid images, not only fire up our imagination but also inspire us and get us excited about our journey of faith.

Recently I received a beautiful calendar from a friend. It is filled with stunning photos of beautiful landscapes that the photographer took in his travels. I am inspired to visit this land just by viewing these pictures. The calendar is filled with pictures of panoramic landscapes of a country in Central Asia that I find difficult to pronounce. Kyrgyzstan, a small country nestled in the high mountains between China and the Asian steppes, aspires to become the "Switzerland" (another metaphor!) of Central Asia. It served as a key transit point along the Silk Road in ancient times. It is obvious that the landscape photographer, Andrew Chen, loved what he saw and wanted to share this beautiful land to the outside world. He writes in his calendar:

The Power of Metaphor

These images are but a sampling of the natural beauty this country has to offer. It is my privilege and joy to be able to share with you the pictures in this calendar. You will always be an honored guest in Kyrgyzstan!

Hopefully what I share in this book, using metaphors to highlight the different landscapes of spiritual formation, will challenge and inspire the reader to travel on an adventurous and exciting journey. Like Andrew, I will like to invite you to be an honored guest in the spiritual "Kyrgyzstan." You can spend time trekking deserts, climbing mountains, rafting rivers, crossing seas, and enjoying gardens. The journey is good for your soul and you will carry on "until Christ is formed in you" (Gal 4:19). Following the example in the Bible, let us begin this journey in the garden.

QUESTIONS TO CONSIDER AND REFLECT

1. Are you aware of the power and pervasive use of metaphors in your life? Can you think of some metaphors that are commonly used without knowing that they are metaphors?
2. Why does the psalmist like to use metaphorical language in his prayers to God? Do you address God using metaphorical language in your prayers?
3. In what ways can metaphors induce you to intuitively and emotionally take sides and get you to involve and participate?
4. Are there places in your life that invoke a certain mood or feeling in you? Why are these places so special in your life?

2

Garden of Growth

The best fertilizer is the gardener's shadow.
—AUTHOR UNKNOWN

GARDEN OF THE SOUL

WE EXPECT FLOWERS TO bloom and trees to grow providing shade or fruit when we plant a garden. We will be disappointed if we have withered flowers and stunted trees in our garden. In the biblical story of the Vine and the Branches, the gardener will cut off every unfruitful branch and prune every fruitful branch so that it will bear more fruit. A dedicated gardener knows the pleasure the garden brings when she can see and enjoy the results of her hard labor. Once I had dinner at a friend's house in Vancouver. It was cold in the evening and steamboat was the perfect choice. He had a vegetable plot in his backyard. He went to his garden plot whenever he needed to add more vegetables into the steaming pot of meat and seafood. He told me that the vegetables planted some time ago were now ready for the table. He obviously took delight in his vegetables by declaring proudly that his homegrown vegetables were organic and free from pesticides. They tasted better when they were plucked directly from the soil and brought to the table for immediate consumption.

God is often pictured as a gardener in the Bible. He planted a garden for Adam to live there. The garden that God planted was perfect: an enclosed garden of lush vegetation, flowing streams, and quiet tranquility. Adam and Eve enjoyed the simple pleasures of life provided by the trees, which were not only pleasing to the eyes but also good for food. The garden, apart from heaven, is the paradisiacal image of human longing on earth. Many people find gardening a great pastime for this reason. They do not mind getting their hands soiled by the moist earth and their body soaked with perspiration under the merciless sun. The dank smell of earth, dead leaves, and manure will not deter them from spending precious time in the garden: planting, potting, weeding, raking, watering, fertilizing, and harvesting. Hours spent in the garden have a therapeutic effect on both the body and soul. The restorative power of a well-grown garden with trees, shrubs, and flowers, is well known. It heals the broken spirit and soothes the frayed nerves. Its colors, smells, sounds, texture bring delight and pleasure to the senses. Ralph Waldo Emerson, a nineteenth-century American poet, has this to say about gardens: "All my hurts my garden spade can heal. A woodland walk, a quest of river-grapes, a mocking thrush, a wild rose, or rock-loving columbine, salve my worst wounds."[1]

Teresa of Avila, the seventeenth-century Carmelite nun, used the image of a garden to illustrate the rhythms of prayer. The plants and flowers in the garden were watered by different kinds of prayers. The fragrant plants and flowers in the garden of the soul are the virtues that bring delight and refreshment to God. This is to invoke God to come often, to fellowship and to take pleasure,

---

1. Griffeth, ed., *The Garden Book of Verse*, 6.

Garden of the Soul

in the garden of the soul.[2] Have you ever wondered about laboring in the garden of your soul? Are you as zealous and passionate working in the garden of your soul as compared to working in your physical garden? Do you give to your soul the proper care and attentiveness like you give to your garden? The neglected soul, like the garden, will be overgrown with thorns, thistles, and nettles. Weeds will thrive and other unwelcomed intruders will creep into the garden to stunt its growth. A garden will not grow by itself if left alone. Much conscious thought and effort must be put into the garden to see it thrive and grow healthily. One day, King Solomon passed by a neglected vineyard and this was what he saw:

> I went past the field of the sluggard, past the vineyard of the man who lacks judgment; thorns had come up everywhere, the ground was covered with weeds, and the stone wall was in ruins. I applied my heart to what I observed and learned a lesson from what I saw; a little sleep, a little slumber, a little folding of the hands to rest—and poverty will come on you like a bandit and scarcity like an armed man. (Prov 24:30–34)

Thomas Moore is the author of the acclaimed book *Care of the Soul*. According to him, a neglected soul is the source of all kinds of problems afflicting us. Our addictions, misplaced passions, obsessions, loss of meaning, and emotional and mental pain are derived from this "loss of soul." Only by caring for the soul will we be able to find solace and help to deal with our addictions, obsessions, and pains. We will be able to discover that life can be meaningful and filled with pleasure and delight through caring for our soul. The opening sentence of his book is revealing and surprises many: "The greatest malady of the twentieth century, implicated in all our troubles and affecting us individually and socially is 'loss of soul.'"[3]

---

2. Chase, *The Tree of Life*, 133–34.
3. Moore, *Care of the Soul*, xi.

CULTIVATION OF THE SOUL: WEEDING

How can we prevent this "loss of soul"? How can we start caring for the soul to ensure its growth? How can we begin the cultivation of the garden of our soul? A good gardener will prepare the soil on the plot that he plans to plant his seeds. He waters the plot daily and sees that it receives sufficient sunlight to grow. From time to time he prunes the plants in order for them to bear more fruit. These steps of weeding, planting, and pruning are essential to the growth of the garden.

The gardener needs to check the condition of the soil first if he plans to plant seeds on his new plot. Any harmful thing in the soil will be taken away for good. All kinds of weeds, thorns, and stones must be removed in order for the plants to grow well. The soil must be in a good condition to receive the seeds. Similarly, we need to examine the condition of our heart in order to grow spiritually. The Bible encourages self-examination: "Search me, O God, and know my heart; test me and know my anxious thoughts. See if there is any offensive way in me, and lead me in the way everlasting" (Ps 139:23–24). Self-examination, though a neglected discipline of the Christian life, is important for two reasons. First, such a discipline leads to knowledge of self. This knowledge in turn awakens our knowledge of God, which is needful for our spiritual growth. Augustine once wrote, "Grant, Lord, that I may know myself and that I may know thee."[4] Second, this discipline will help us identify and cope with the temptations of the flesh. These temptations will awaken our passions to sin if we fail to control these desires. These passions will hinder our spiritual growth because they prevent the work of God's grace in our life.

According to the teachings of the desert monks in the fourth century, humans are afflicted with eight "deadly thoughts" that are modeled after the temptations of Christ in the wilderness. These thoughts will stir up the unruly passions in us to sin against God if we do not master them. They are considered deadly not because they are worst than the sins of murder or theft but because they

---

4. Augustine, *Soliloquies*, 2.1, quoted in Chan, *Spiritual Theology*, 153.

predispose us to sin. These thoughts are universally experienced by most people. These passions when aroused will distract us from spiritual matters and will make us feeble and inattentive to God's presence in our life. We cannot grow spiritually without God working in us. This is pointed out by Richard Foster in his celebrated book *Celebration of Discipline*. He writes, "The needed change within us is God's work, not ours. The demand is for an inside job, and only God can work from the inside."[5] According to Evagrius, a fourth-century monastic scholar, these are the eight thoughts: gluttony, lust, greed, sadness, anger, apathy, vainglory, and pride.[6]

We eat what we want and not what we need in our affluent society. It is easy to go overboard in our consumption of food. Gluttony leads to overeating and obesity has become a serious social problem for the younger generation who are addicted to fast food. Paul reminds us not to let the stomach be our god. We need to limit ourselves to what is necessary and not what is desirable. It takes discipline and effort on our part not to over-indulge in a world where food consumption is no longer a necessity but a favorite pastime.

The second thought is lust. Lust is different from love because love honors the person and treats the body of the person with respect. Lust desires to make use of the person's body for sexual gratification. Lust violates the person's dignity and honor by treating the body as an object. A good example is Amnon, the son of David. He loved Tamar, the beautiful sister of Absalom. Amnon feigned illness and planned to have Tamar come to his room to attend to him. When David came to visit him, he requested for Tamar to come over to his place and make some special bread for him to eat. David consented and sent word to Tamar to help her brother. Tamar came with the bread and brought it to Amnon's bedroom. Amnon took this opportunity to rape her and then told her to get out of his sight. He hated her more than he loved her

5. Quoted in Kang, *Deep-Rooted in Christ*, 68.

6. I am indebted to Diogenes Allen for this section on Evagrius' eight deadly thoughts. See his book *Spiritual Theology*, 67–78.

after violating his sister. Apparently, Amnon's "love" for Tamar was just pure lust (2 Sam 13).

The third thought is greed for material gain. According to Evagrius, we hoard earthly goods to guarantee a secure future. Then we will not need to depend on others or go begging for help when we grow old. We want to be prepared and ready for any eventual crisis in our life: sickness, famine, unemployment, prolonged old age. It is easy to think that we can secure our future with material wealth. The parable of the Rich Fool serves as a warning to those who covet such thoughts. One day a rich man has an abundant harvest. He has so much possession that he decides to build a bigger place to store up his wealth. He can now take life easy because he is confident that his wealth can last for a long time. He is heard saying to himself, "You have plenty of good things laid up for many years. Take life easy; eat, drink and be merry." The rich fool does not know that he cannot enjoy his wealth for long. God says to him, "You fool! This very night your life will be demanded from you" (Luke 12:13–21).

The fourth thought is sadness. Most of us do not think that sadness can be a hindrance or temptation to our spiritual life. Evagrius thinks otherwise. This sadness is actually a form of self-pity. When we compare ourselves with others who are doing much better than us we become sad or disappointed. At the same time, we believe that we can only be happy if things or circumstances are different. Consequently, we look to people or things to give us joy instead of looking to God. We entertain the idea that if not for our obedience to the gospel work, we would be enjoying the pleasures of the world just like our friends and neighbors. This is the devil's ploy to cause us to feel sad or wallow in self-pity. We need to overcome this by learning the secret of contentment despite the circumstances.

The fifth thought is anger. Sadness and disappointment will provide the stage for anger to birth and flourish. According to Evagrius, this anger is caused by injury or hurt that we receive. We bear a grudge against those who hurt us with unkind remarks or unjust actions. The very thought of these people will fill us with an inner rage that can easily burst out into a fiery passion of angry words or actions. This is the reason why we need to deal with our anger the moment we detect it simmering inside us. It is wise to take heed of Paul's words when he writes that we "do not let the sun go down while we are still angry." Uncontrolled anger can be used by the devil to gain a foothold in our life and to cause us to sin (Eph 4:26–27).

The sixth thought is apathy or sloth. We experience apathy when we hit a plateau in our spiritual life. Spiritual inertia takes over, and we lack the passion or desire to come out of the spiritual rut. We begin to lose interest in spiritual matters and become lazy. At the same time, we tend to find fault with the church and other Christians. Spiritual laziness or apathy is condemned in the parable of the Talents by Jesus in the New Testament. In this parable three servants are given talents of money to invest. The servant with the one talent decides to hide it in the ground while the other two use their talents to earn more money. The servant with the one talent is condemned by the master for not investing his money to earn more talents (Matt 25:14–30).

The seventh thought is vainglory. Unlike apathy, vainglory takes place when we think that we are doing well spiritually. We think that we are better than others and want people to notice our spiritual progress. We will take every opportunity to promote ourselves before others because we want others to think highly of us. The last thought is pride. Evagrius saw the difference between vainglory and pride. Pride is when the self takes over the place of God and not giving him the credit for his spiritual advancement. Pride, like vainglory, makes us feel superior to others. We exalt ourselves by putting others down. It was Gregory the Great who identified that pride is the source of the other seven sins. It is the root sin. To Augustine, pride is the beginning of sin. It is "undue exaltation, when the soul abandons him to whom it ought to cleave

Garden of Growth

as its end, and becomes a kind of end to itself."[7] Since then, many came to view pride as the beginning of the seven deadly sins. The list was subsequently shortened to seven when vainglory and pride were put together as one sin instead of two.

We are distracted from focusing on spiritual matters by these deadly thoughts. Instead of staying focused and attentive to God, our mind is pulled in different directions by competing desires. Our attention, according to Simeon Weil, is the only faculty of soul that gives us access to God.[8] The Greek word for the desert monk is *monachos*, which means "single" or "undivided." Diogenes Allen, who teaches at Princeton Theology Seminary, writes:

> The *monachos* has interior unity or purity of heart, bringing the whole self to focus on God and to desire God as the sole treasure. Unless we can bring our scattered thoughts and feelings into focus, we cannot see or understand ourselves, our neighbor, or the created universe, nor can we proceed from this indirect knowledge to direct knowledge of God face-to-face.[9]

How can we stay focused and achieve interior unity or purity of heart? How can we gather our thoughts and feelings together and be attentive? Having a "rule of life" can help us to stay focused. I will talk more about this rule of life later in the chapter. Evagrius also mentioned the need for solitude as a means to extinguish the flames of desire.[10] Solitude and silence is a discipline to help us attain the gift of attentiveness. I will talk about this discipline in a later chapter. I have written on this subject of solitude and silence in my book *Being Truly Human*. This book takes inspiration from the desert monks of the fourth and fifth centuries. It challenges fellow Christians to begin a spiritual odyssey, in the desert of their soul, in order to become their true selves. The practice of solitude and silence will lead them to be indifferent to the crying needs of

---

7. Augustine, *City of God*, 2:237.
8. Quoted in Allen, *Spiritual Theology*, 82.
9. Ibid., 81.
10. Ibid., 83.

25

their false selves in order to give God their undivided attention, which is needed for the spiritual formation of their true selves.

CULTIVATION OF THE SOUL: PLANTING

As a good gardener of our own soul, we need to take the first step of preparing the soil to receive God's grace. We need to identify the deadly thoughts and have control over their unruly passions. As suggested by Paul, one way to turn our minds away from these deadly thoughts is to think about what is true, noble, right, pure, lovely, admirable, excellent, and praiseworthy. To put these thoughts into action will reinforce them in our minds (Phil 3:8–9). We need to make sure that the condition of the soil is good and free from all kinds of hindrances so that it is ready to receive God's grace. The next step is to make sure that our plants are well nourished by water and light. Rain and sunlight are God's gifts to us. The garden cannot grow without God blessing the earth. The reason we give thanks and say grace each time we eat is to acknowledge that all good things come from God who blesses the earth with rain and light. While we do our part to grow a fruitful garden, growth ultimately comes from God (1 Cor 3:6–7). We need to team up with God and rely on his grace if our souls are to grow and bear fruit.

Once there was a village organist who gave a recital in a church. In those days church organs needed someone to pump the wind into the instrument and the person was usually hidden behind the curtain near to the organ. After each item the organist would rise and bow to acknowledge the applause given by the audience. He would say, "Now I will play the next piece, which is . . ." (he then named it). Returning to the stool after the bow he put his fingers on the keys but no sound came. He tried again with the same result. After a while, a boy peered from behind the curtain and said, "Let's have a little more 'we' in it."[11]

---

11. Hughes, *7 Laws of Spiritual Success*, 170.

Garden of Growth

Everyone knows that plants in the garden need water for growth. A tree planted by streams of water is a picture of fruitfulness and growth. It will yield its seasonal fruit and its leaf will remain green all year round. Water is a scarce resource in a semi-arid land where rainfall is marginal and subject to seasonal changes. It is not strange that water is a common topic in the Bible. The conversation centered on the subject of water when Jesus met the Samaritan woman at the well. The woman was interested in the "living water" that Jesus was talking about. Drawing and fetching water from well to home was laborious work. She would not be thirsty and have to keep coming to draw water if she had this "living water." Jericho was the first city in Canaan that came under the sword of Joshua. Joshua captured Jericho for its strategic supply of abundant water. Jericho was called a "city of palms" because it was located below sea level around a huge natural spring. Likewise, Jerusalem served well as a fortress city because of its water supply tapped from a spring nearby. This could be a strategic reason why David chose Jerusalem as his capital.

The provision of rain was God's covenant promise to bless the people of Israel. He would send rain to bless the earth if Israel faithfully obeyed God's commands to love and serve him with heart and soul. "So if you faithfully obey the commands I am giving you today . . . then I will send rain on your land in its season, both autumn and spring rains, so that you may gather in your grain, new wine and oil. I will provide grass in the fields for your cattle, and you will eat and be satisfied." If Israel disobeyed by bowing down and worship other gods, God would "shut the heavens so that it will not rain and the ground will yield no produce, and you will soon perish from the good land the Lord is giving you" (Deut 11:13-15; 16-17). Water is a blessing from God, and a lack of it is a curse from God.

Jacob called his sons to gather around him so that he could bless them when he was about to die. Jacob blessed Joseph that he would be a "fruitful vine near a spring, whose branches climb over a wall." He assured Joseph that God would bless him by the "blessings of the heavens above, blessings of the deep that lies below" (Gen 49:22, 25). It is clear that rain and spring water were seen as blessings from God to favor Joseph and to ensure his future prosperity.

Besides water, sunlight is an essential component for plants to grow and flourish as well. My wife has some plants around the house. She will move the plants around to ensure that they get adequate light throughout the year due to the seasonal changes in the sun's direction. Certain plants require more light than other plants. Some grow better with diffused light while others thrive under strong light. We also know that humans too need a good dose of natural and artificial light for our well-being. Winter is usually the season when people get depressed because they are exposed to less sunlight. According to Thomas Wehr, a research psychologist on the effects of the environment on human behavior, one way to fight depression is to expose ourselves to outdoor light and spend less time indoors. An hour's walk in the neighborhood will help to fight depression. He says:

> The waiting rooms at SAD (season affective depression) clinics empty out if we get a few anomalous springlike days in February, probably because people attracted outdoors by the balmy air end up getting more light, which activates them and fights depression.[12]

Light, as opposed to darkness, is deemed to be from God. The first creative act of God was to call forth light. Jesus says that he is the light of the world. John says that God is light and in heaven there will be no more sun or lamp to give light for God himself will give light to us. Light represents goodness and holiness. To be under God's light, according to the psalmist, is to be blessed. "Who can show us any good? Let the light of your face shine upon us, O Lord" (Ps 4:6). The Aaronic benediction to bless Israel also calls upon God's light to shine upon his people. "The Lord bless you and keep you; the Lord make his face shine upon you and be

---

12. Gallagher, *The Power of Place*, 45.

gracious to you; the Lord turn his face toward you and give you peace" (Num 6:24–26).

CULTIVATION OF THE SOUL: PRUNING

God, out of his grace, sends the rain to water the earth and the sun to give light. The garden of our soul begins to grow and bear fruit when exposed to God's grace. A third stage is necessary in the cultivation of the soul. The branches need pruning to produce more fruit. Pruning also gets rid of those unwanted branches that are dead or diseased and helps to give the plant a better shape as well. Pruning is not easy for the gardener because she has watched the plant grow over time from tiny twigs to full branches. It is daunting for her but the job needs to be done in order to produce bigger blossoms and more fruit.

The garden of our soul needs pruning. God disciplines us so that we can share in his holiness and grow into spiritual maturity. It is out of his love as Father that he disciplines us. Growth is painful. As we mature in life we go through a series of different stages. At each transition we experience pain due to a sense of loss. We need to live with it because it is part of growing up. I remember the first time I attended school. The classroom was a strange world for me. Mum was there with me on my first day of class. I got nervous when I could not see my mum on the second day of class. She had to work and was not able to stay back at school. I kept looking outside to catch a glimpse of her. She was not there. I tried to put up a brave front while other kids in the class were crying for their parents. Mum was no longer taking me to school after the first week. It was a scary experience to walk to school by myself but I got over it. That was the first of the many transitions of life that I had to take. Each transition was painful but necessary for personal growth.

God will bring situations in our life that can be painful but necessary for our spiritual development. Every saint of God can testify to this. God may want us to let go of something or someone that we hold dear and close to our heart. It is painful to let go. Conversely, God may want us to accept a situation or person that we may not like. It is equally painful to accept the unpleasant. Take for example the "thorn" of Paul. We are not sure what this "thorn" means but we know that Paul would rather not have it with him. Three times he prayed for it to be removed but each time the answer from God was negative. He had to live with it. This weakness in Paul's life led him to experience the power of God working in him. Paul said that he would rather boast in his weakness caused by the "thorn" so that the power of Christ might rest on him (2 Cor 12:7–10).

RULE OF LIFE

Certain plants need some structure for support in order for them to grow. We know that tomatoes grow on stakes, beans on strings, and creeping vines on walls or trellis. A structure like the trellis enables the vine to get off the ground, grow upwards to catch the light, and become more productive. We, like the plants, need structure and support to grow spiritually. We need a "rule of life" to grow freely. In fact the English word for "rule" comes from the Greek word for "trellis." It is an intentional and conscious effort on our part to have a plan for growth. I find the description by Peter Scazzero helpful:

> A rule of life, very simply, is an intentional, conscious plan to keep God at the center of everything we do. It provides guidelines to help us continually remember God as the Source of our lives. It includes our unique combination of spiritual practices that provide structure and direction for us to intentionally pay attention and remember God in everything we do. The starting point and foundation of any rule is a desire to be with God and to love him.[13]

---

13. Scazzero, *Emotionally Healthy Spirituality*, 196.

Garden of Growth

We need a rule to help us stay focused and be attentive to God in our life. A rule consists of a series of selected practices that we observe on a daily or regular basis that keep us on course for growth. Without a rule all our desires and aspirations for growth will not happen. We need a rule to manage these practices so that through time they become a part of us. The regular and repeated use of these practices will set a rhythm and orientation in our life to help us maintain our spiritual focus. They are considered as disciplines when these practices have become a habitual life pattern. A rule requires commitment on our part to keep it. A well-designed rule will only be on paper and will not take off anytime without a desire and commitment to grow spiritually.

A rule may not be too restrictive or overbearing. When deciding on a rule we need to prayerfully consider certain criteria that make up a good rule. It must not be too ambitious but something that is doable and within reach. We need to see how this rule fits into our pattern of living and daily routine without making too much change to it. We need to know our personal limitations and be realistic about our commitment level. It is not necessary to apply a rule fully at first. We may want to take baby steps and implement each discipline provisionally as we move along. It is good to grow into it rather than having it forced on us. We may stumble on a rule that truly suits our needs after some time.

We need to select our disciplines carefully and see how they can help us in our spiritual growth. Not all disciplines are "spiritual" in nature. Some have to do with our eating habits, physical exercise, sleeping routine, abstinence, and solitary walks. Other familiar disciplines are Scripture reading, study of books on spirituality, prayer, fasting, spiritual reading of the Bible and other classical books, solitude and silence, retreats, worship, and many more. It is important to know that not all disciplines incorporated in a rule need to be done individually. Some disciplines can be observed corporately. It is also advisable to consider certain disciplines that may be less appealing but can give us greater growth than the familiar ones that we find attractive.

This rule can work against us if we are careless. We must not think that our life will be transformed just by having a rule of life. A rule is not an end but a means to an end. This rule can be used wrongly to win God's favor, to get God working for us according to our plans, to grow our life spiritually based on our own efforts, to impress other people of our spirituality or to win acceptance by others.[14] We need to check ourselves in order to know the reason for such a rule of life. Is it practiced out of love and obedience to God? Is it our deep desire to grow in knowing God that we are committed to this rule?

It is not an easy task to implement a rule of life. Our initial efforts may be disappointing, and we may not be successful on our first launch. There will be many hiccups and breakdowns along the way and things may not go well as planned. We need to be patient and not give up easily. We will be able to see the results if we persevere over time. Meanwhile, God's grace will be sufficient for us to keep going and growing. John Wesley cautions us that we need a rule of life, whether we like it or not, for it is the means for us to grow:

> O, Begin! Fix some part of every day for private exercises . . . Whether you like it or not, read and pray daily. It is for your life; there is no other way: else you will be trifler all your days . . . Do justice to your own soul; give it time and means to grow. Do not starve yourself anymore.[15]

THE PROCESS OF GROWTH

Growth is a process and takes time. What do we see when we cut a cross-section of a tree trunk? We see rings on it that signify the number of years it takes for the tree to grow to its present stage. The more mature trees have many more rings on its trunk. We notice that each ring varies in width if we study the rings carefully. The width of the ring indicates the growth rate of the tree for that

---

14. Mulholland, *Invitation to a Journey*, 104.
15. Thompson, *Soul Feast*, 145.

Garden of Growth

particular year. Some rings are much narrower than the others indicating a negative year of growth for the tree. Not only growth takes time but is uneven as well. The tree experiences spurts of growth in some years and is lean in others. We also know that spiritual growth follows the pattern of physical growth.

Growth, in the modern society, is facilitated by know-how or techniques. The poultry industry is a good example. It normally takes over two months for chickens to reach their weight that is suitable for the dining table. These chickens roam freely in the farm with plenty of time to exercise and to feed on the grass. A chicken can grow to a marketable size within forty days with the use of growth hormone in the feed. Farmed chickens, as opposed to free-range chickens, are packed in a congested, enclosed space with little room to move, in order to gain weight faster. A free-range chicken is healthier and tasted better though it costs more than a farmed chicken. A farmed chicken has more fat and water in its meat.

There is no proven technique or shortcut in growing our spiritual life. The process can be tedious and difficult and we are tempted to give up with the thought that spiritual maturity is only for a small group of spiritually elite people. At times we feel abandoned by God as we enter a period of spiritual dryness when God is hidden in darkness and nowhere near us. We lose the passion and desire for God and the things in the world. A sense of failure sinks in and we are tempted to give up pursuing after holiness in our life. The initial euphoria has subsided and we begin to have negative feelings about our journey with God. At this stage we must remember not to get impatient or fretful. We need to persevere through this dark period because this is the time when God is doing his divine work of grace in areas beyond our knowing and consciousness. John of the Cross, a sixteenth-century Carmelite friar and priest, has these words for us:

> Oh, then, spiritual soul, when you see your appetites darkened, your inclinations dry and constrained, your faculties incapacitated for any interior exercise, do not be

> afflicted; think of this as a grace, since God is freeing you from yourself and taking you from your own activity.[16]

Some people may think that they can exercise the option to take it or leave it since spiritual growth is a tedious and difficult process. This quest for a more holy life with God will suit certain groups of people and is not for everybody. Robert Muholland, author and professor of New Testament, points out that we are all shaped spiritually. We are shaped in our being by our actions, thoughts, relationships, emotions, responses, and reactions. We are either transformed into a more wholesome character bearing Christ's image or deformed into a character that is broken and destructive. We really have no choice, for life itself is a process of spiritual development for all of us. He writes:

> Spiritual formation is not an option! The inescapable conclusion is that life itself is a process of spiritual development. The only choice we have is whether that growth moves us toward wholeness in Christ or toward an increasingly dehumanized and destructive mode of being.[17]

To grow in our love for God and for others is to grow spiritually. Love is the primary virtue in the nine-fold fruit of the Holy Spirit (Gal 5:22-23). For Augustine, living the sanctified life requires us to exercise the four virtues of temperance, prudence, fortitude, and justice with love for God as the object. According to him, temperance is love keeping itself entire and uncorrupted for God; fortitude is love bearing everything readily for the sake of God; justice is love serving God only, and therefore ruling well all else, as subject to man; prudence is love making a right decision between what helps it towards God and what might hinder it.[18] Spiritual growth takes place in the midst of relationships between us, God, and others. We know that we are growing spiritually when the quality of our relationship with God and with others improves.

16. John of the Cross, *The Collected Works*, 365.
17. Mulholland, *Invitation*, 24.
18. Augustine, *On the Morals of the Catholic Church*, 4:48.

We know that we have made progress in our spiritual life when we are more loving, more caring, more patient, more forgiving, and more understanding than before.[19]

Conclusion

The garden of our soul needs tending. The garden will not bear fruit without intentional and conscious effort to work the soil. The steps of weeding, planting, and pruning are essential to the growth of the garden. We need to examine our life in order to weed the garden of those thoughts that give rise to our carnal desires to sin against God. Turning our minds from the things of this world to the things of God will help to achieve this. The next step is to make sure that the plants receive adequate sunlight and water. Rain and sunlight are God's gifts to us. Likewise, we need to rely on God's grace if our souls are to grow and bear fruit. Our soul needs pruning in order to bear more fruit. God's discipline is painful at times but perseverance will bear results. Certain plants need some structure and support in order for them to grow. A rule of life, which consists of selected practices that we observe regularly, will provide the necessary support and structure for us to stay focused and be attentive to God. Spiritual growth, like physical growth, takes time and the process can be tedious and difficult but the grace of God will see us through. We will enjoy the good times and also the lean times as we grow spiritually. We know we are growing spiritually when we are growing in our relationship with God and others.

QUESTIONS TO CONSIDER AND REFLECT

1. When you think of a garden as a metaphor for your soul, what comes to your mind and what is your response?

---

19. Mulholland, *Invitation*, 42.

Garden of the Soul

2. If you are the gardener of your soul, where should you begin work to make the garden a delight to the eyes and a pleasure to the heart of God?

3. Do you have a rule of life? What are the challenges you will personally face if you want to implement and maintain a rule of life?

4. Identify one or more of the eight "deadly thoughts" that stir up the unruly passions in you and predispose you to sin against God. Explain how you propose to deal with these thoughts in your life now.

3

River of Life

It occurs to me, thinking about prayer, that most of the time I get the direction wrong. I start downstream with my own concerns and bring them to God. I inform God as if God did not already know. I plead with God, as if hoping to change God's mind and overcome divine reluctance. Instead, I should start upstream where the flow begins.
—PHILIP YANCEY[1]

LIFE-GIVING PRAYER

ONCE I WAS IN a small village that was situated at the first bend of the Yangtze River in Yunnan, China. At this juncture, the Yangtze makes a u-turn, going north instead of flowing south. It will flow through Indo-China if the river continues to flow south. The Yangtze, or *Chang Jiang* in Chinese, is the largest river in China and the third longest in the world. Its discharge by volume is the biggest in the world. It begins its four-thousand-mile journey

---

1. Yancey, *Prayer*, 15.

37

from the glaciers of the Tanggula Mountains in Qinghai Province, and running eastward, the river pours into the East China Sea at Shanghai. The mighty river drains one fifth of the land area in China, and its river basin is home to one third of the country's population. A village teacher of a local school took us to a government building located on top of a hill. From that vantage point we enjoyed a panoramic view of the river and could see the rooftops of the entire village just below us. The pastoral landscape was stunningly beautiful. The river looked tranquil and peaceful at this early stage of its journey. It has been used as a lifeline for millions of people for purposes of irrigation, transportation, sanitation, and even industry for centuries. It has a notorious reputation of overflowing its banks and causing widespread floods and hardships for many. I had a sudden urge to go down the hill and see the river at close range. I told my friend that we must make a quick trip to the river bank before leaving the village. I wanted to touch its life-giving waters knowing that it had touched many lives for good or bad since ancient times.

Rivers, like gardens, appeal to many people. The river's water is perceived as a source of life. The river is used as a symbol of God's presence in the Bible. The river that runs through Jerusalem is used to image the presence of God by the psalmist (Ps 46:4–5). Ezekiel's temple has a river running through it which again symbolizes God's presence (Ezek 47:1). Jesus uses the image of "rivers of living water" to refer to the Holy Spirit (John 7:38–39). The river of the water of life flows from the throne running down the main street of the holy city in the New Jerusalem (Rev 22:1–2). Rivers, like mountains, are used in the Bible as places of divine encounters. God's voice from heaven declares Jesus as God's Son at the River Jordan (Mark 1:9–11). Ezekiel sees visions of God by the River Kebar in Babylon (Ezek 1:1). Daniel too sees a vision of an angelic being, sent from heaven, while standing at the bank of the River Tigris in Babylon (Dan 10:4–6). Paul expects to find a place of prayer by a river located outside the city gate of Philippi (Acts 16:13).

River of Life

Prayer is the lifeline of our spiritual life just as the river is a lifeline for many whose livelihood is dependent on it. Prayer, according to Henri Nouwen, is the most basic movement of the spiritual life. No man or woman hopes to stay spiritually alive without the need to pray for it is the very breath of life. Prayer is "the basic receptive attitude out of which all of life can receive new vitality."[2] Prayer is the life sign of our faith just as breathing is a clear sign of being alive. Like the cry of a baby, prayer comes naturally to us the moment we are born spiritually. It is the first act that ushers us into God's kingdom when we become a part of Christ's body. It is also the one act on which all our other spiritual exercises depend.[3] Fasting is practiced in the context of prayer, while meditation leads to a prayerful response. Reading of Scripture will result in prayer of obedience, and self-examination will lead to prayer of confession. Prayer not only saturates everything that we do in life but redeems every aspect of our life as well. It is the key link in our engagement with God. No wonder Paul calls on Christians to practice the art of unceasing prayer (1 Thess 5:17).

Unceasing prayer is like the constant flow of the river. I came across numerous wadis or dry riverbeds during the dry season in Nepal. Wadis are used by many Nepalese as routes for transportation during the dry season. Such crossings can be dangerous when sudden but infrequent heavy rainfall can cause flash floods. A catastrophic and sudden flash flood on the River Seti, which was near to the tourist town of Pokara, caused the death of fifteen people and thirty-six missing including three Ukrainian tourists on May 5, 2012. The flow of the rivers is dependent on the melting glaciers from the mountains and the periodic rains. Many places are impoverished for lack of water due to the lack of perennial rivers that flow throughout the year. The region remains poor and unproductive. Our spiritual life is unproductive and impoverished if our prayers, like the many rivers in Nepal, are irregular and intermittent. How then can we pray unceasingly?

---

2. Nouwen, *Reaching Out*, 114, 133.
3. Chan, *Spiritual Theology*, 127.

PRAYING UNCEASINGLY

Unceasing prayer is possible because of the Holy Spirit that dwells in us. "God is not far from each of us," said Paul, "and in him we live and move and have our being" (Acts 17:28). What we lack is a desire for God's presence. Not everything can be prayer but everything can become prayer if we develop a habit of giving loving attention to God's presence in our daily life.[4] Most of us will find difficulty in thinking about God all the time or to pray constantly with heads bowed, knees bended, or hands raised. Unceasing prayer is more than just a religious act. It is a posture or way of life that we consciously adopt when we desire to submit every part of our life to God. We need to develop an awareness of his presence in different aspects of our life in order to make prayer a way of life. It is to live our entire life in the presence of God.

Brother Lawrence, a lay brother in a Carmelite monastery, worked in the kitchen. Brother Lawrence, while working, turned his attention to God by opening himself to his presence in the midst of his busy life. He did not wait for the hour of prayer to arrive before he turned to God. God was as real to him in the kitchen as it was in the chapel. In fact Lawrence found the usual forms of formal prayers and meditations not working well for him. To Lawrence, God's presence was everywhere and he could converse with him at all times of the day. He said:

> The time of business does not with me differ from the time of prayer; and in the noise and clatter of my kitchen, while several persons are at the same time calling for different things; I possess God in as great tranquility as if I were upon my knees at the Blessed Sacrament.[5]

Anything that draws our attention to God is prayer. A beautiful sunset or a flight of birds gliding towards the horizon can lead us to praise God for his amazing handiwork. We need to appreciate the senses that God has given us: the ability to see, touch, smell, hear, and taste has greatly enriched our life. We feel deprived and

---

4. Chase, *The Tree of Life*, 19.
5. Lawrence, *Practice of the Presence of God*, 20.

inadequate the moment we lose one of these senses. Anything that we can see, touch, taste, hear or smell in the daily activities of our life can be used as a prayer to God.[6] We can trace the presence of the divine in our world through them. Anything around us can become prayer if we pay attention and be able to catch a glimpse of the divine in these things. Our senses open a door to the reality of God around us. It is impossible not to catch a glimpse of God unless we harden our hearts. Bonaventure, in his book *The Soul Journey*, makes this point:

> Whoever, therefore, is not enlightened by such splendor of created things is blind; whoever is not awakened by such outcries is deaf; whoever does not praise God because of all these effects is dumb; whoever does not discover the First Principle from such clear signs is a fool.[7]

A warm hug from someone we have not met for a long time, the fragrant smell of flowers in spring, the sound of children laughing and playing joyously in a park, the sight of the River Yangtze winding its way through the hills and patches of rice fields, and the taste of our favorite food can open ourselves to God and lead us in conversation with God. We can use moments like these to encounter God. Moments like these should cause us to pause and take time to acknowledge his presence in our life.

Saint Benedict, founder of Western monasticism, taught his monks that the ordinary was the divine and the divine ordinary. "The divine is everywhere. It's just as much in the smell of the hay or the faces on the bus or the petals of a daisy as it is in the majesty of the mountains or the tranquility of a cathedral."[8] Nothing is more ordinary and mundane than work: tedious, boring, and routine. Yet, to the Benedictine monk, work can be liberating and a means to meet the divine. "To work is to pray" is a phrase often quoted by the monks to view work not as a means for profit or productivity but to be co-creators with the divine and an arena to en-

---

6. Benner, *Opening to God*, 76–78.
7. Bonaventure, *The Soul's Journey to God*, 67.
8. Bell, *A Subtle and Deep Joy*, x–xi.

counter God on a daily basis. To the Benedictine monk, work has a purpose and is not a time-filler or a way to make money. Work, according to Joan Chittister, a Benedictine nun, is co-creative and is "what we do to continue what God wanted done" in his world.[9]

TOO BUSY TO PRAY

We spend a large chunk of our time working during the day. It is not easy for us who are busy working to pray unceasingly as suggested. This is a difficult discipline because we tend to resist submitting our work to God. It is, as Nouwen notes, "an ongoing struggle against idolatry."[10] It calls for strict obedience which many of us find it hard to follow. The workplace is the arena where we can easily succumb to idolatry because it is where we feel most competent. At work, we are able to exercise control and use our skills and strategies to perform a task. If we are not careful our work can become our idol. God enacted Sabbath to remind us that we are not in control but he is. We can, perhaps, learn from the monks on how not to let work hinder us from the habit of praying unceasingly.

The monks have the habit of praying and singing the Psalms while they work. This habit of turning to God while working is to ensure that their labor is aimed at the pleasure of God. Prayer reminds the monks that work is not self-serving but aims at serving God. It is not mainly for profit or productivity. Rather, work is viewed primarily as playing a role in "furthering the blessings of creation and counter the effects of wickedness."[11] The monks pray to God thanking him for granting strength and wisdom to their hands and minds and for providing the materials used in their work. In so doing, the monks not only feel that they can do their work successfully but also fulfill their duty to pray unceasingly as admonished by the apostle Paul.

---

9. Chittister, *Wisdom Distilled from the Daily*, 86.
10. Nouwen, *Clowning in Rome*, 75.
11. Peterson, *Earth and Altar*, 129.

River of Life

Not all of us have the luxury to sing, pray, and work at the same time. We live in a hurried world crowded with perennial activities that we hardly find the time or space for God in our life. How then can we think and live in God's presence throughout the busy day? Anthony Bloom, in his book *Beginning to Pray*, has found the answer to this dilemma.[12] He was a doctor before he became the Metropolitan of Western Europe. As a physician his aim was to clear, as quickly as possible, the long line of patients waiting at his clinic. He would think of the next patient in the queue while treating one patient and counting the number of those still waiting in his clinic. He was not able to recollect the people that he had examined at the end of the day. Disturbed by this, he decided to change his approach: treating the current patient as the only one in his clinic. He would deliberately force himself, when pressed for time, to slow down and to engage in small talk with the patient for a couple more minutes. He purposed to focus his attention in the present moment and not on the future. He found, to his surprise, that time passed quickly and the inner tension disappeared completely. This method of stopping time when one was pressed to hurry helped transformed Bloom's life.

Bloom had learned the habit of stopping his work at certain times and just sitting in his chair doing nothing for a few minutes. He would say to himself, "I am here in the presence of God, in my own presence and in the presence of all the furniture that is around me, just still, moving nowhere." These short intervals were so relieving that he decided to prolong the time a bit longer. He found that these intervals helped him to get on with his tasks quickly and calmly. He began his day with a prolonged quiet time before God acknowledging that the new day was God's gift and claiming the day for God. He would have another period of quiet time at the end of a busy day to review all that had happened to him. Since the day was gone, he would commit the day to God's gracious hand and learned to rest in him. Philip Yancey, in his book *Prayer: Does It Make Any Difference?*, has this to say about Anthony Bloom:

---

12. Story told by Yancey in his book *Prayer*, 289–92. See Anthony Bloom, *Beginning to Pray*.

> Intervals of stillness and prayer became for Bloom a series of markers strung together like pearls in a necklace, reminding him of the true nature of reality. Life is not a meaningless sequence of actions but an arena in which to live out the will of another world, the kingdom of heaven. Prayer is a state as much as an act, a fact that easily gets forgotten when we confine it to one or two isolated instances a day.[13]

GROWTH IN PRAYER

The river, fed by numerous streams flowing into it, gets deeper and more powerful as the volume of water increases. The river has reached its optimal potential in terms of its use for irrigation, sanitation, transport, and industry at its later stages. It is able to sustain a greater population at this stage of the river's life. We expect a thriving river to grow bigger and stronger as it makes its way to the sea. Like a river's flow, we too expect our prayer life to grow and its potential to affect the lives of others increases.

We enter into a relationship with God through prayer. We also grow in holiness as we grow in this relationship. God says that we are to be holy as he is holy (1 Pet 1:15-16). The goal of prayer is a sanctified relationship with God, and he is calling us to join him in the work of transforming our life. Luke Bell, a Benedictine monk, explains:

> Holiness is our goal in the monastery. In all our labors, whether they are outdoors for the husbandry of our land or inside in the silence of our cells seeking to allow God to speak to us through the sacred texts, we are working toward holiness. Holiness is being fully open to the joy of God. Man is made for holiness.[14]

---

13. Ibid., 291.
14. Bell, *A Deep and Subtle Joy*, 1.

River of Life

Prayer is hard work, as Chan points out, because intimacy with God is difficult.[15] It is difficult because we are relating to a holy God who is perfect and faultless. Each time the relationship gets into trouble the fault lies in us and not in God. We cannot fault God for a relationship that is going through a dry patch or has turned sour. We can only humble ourselves, ask for forgiveness, and seek reconciliation. Every relationship goes through cycles of ups and downs, separation and reconciliation, self-sacrifice and self-centeredness. The intimate relationship between the beloved and lover as portrayed in the Song of Songs carries the wounds of separation and joys of reconciliation:

> I opened for my lover, but my lover had left; he was gone. My heart sank at his departure. I looked for him but did not find him. I called him but he did not answer. (Song 5:6)

> Come, my lover, let us go to the countryside, let us spend the night in the villages. Let us go early to the vineyards to see if the vines have budded, if their blossoms have opened, and if the pomegranates are in bloom—there I will give you my love. (Song 7:11–13)

Forgiveness and reconciliation are necessary to maintain and grow the prayer relationship. Growth in prayer life is similar to growth in marital life.[16] Prayer life is easygoing at the honeymoon stage. Our faith is hardly challenged and our prayers are readily heard and answered. God, like the farmer who is protective over his seedlings from the elements, is there to shelter us with his grace and favor to ensure that we are not hindered in our spiritual growth at the infant stage. The honeymoon period will not last. The protection is taken away when the seedlings have taken root and are able to withstand the force of the natural elements. Prayer becomes a daily struggle when we discover the painful realities of a relationship that needs mending and renewing like a fisherman's net. We begin to doubt his love for us as he seems hidden and far

---

15. Chan, *Spiritual Theology*, 132.
16. Ibid., 134.

away. The temptations get stronger and harder to overcome as we begin to lose the desire for intimacy with God. Distractions get in the way for a deeper life with God. We must not get alarmed or bewildered by such experiences. This process is necessary for our spiritual maturation because growth has to go through the painful process of trials and temptations. Perseverance is needed at this point. A deeper intimacy and more mature love will emerge when we come out of this process. We find that our prayers are focused more on God and less on self. They are less vocal and more mental in the sense that "the one praying engages God with a simple attention of the mind and an equally simple application of the will."[17] It is also easier for us to forgive and seek reconciliation in our relationship with others.

PRAYER IS RISKY BUSINESS

We know that it is easier to flow with the river's current than crossing it. Water was seen flowing from the temple and under its threshold in Ezekiel's vision of the temple. It soon became a river. A man was seen using a measuring rod to measure the river's length. At intervals of 450 meters he would ask Ezekiel to wade across the river at this point. At first the river was ankle-deep. Then it was knee-deep. Further down the river it was up to the waist of Ezekiel. At a further point the prophet found it impossible to wade across anymore because at this point the water was too deep to cross. It was deep enough to swim in it. When Ezekiel was led to the river's bank and was no longer focused on crossing the swift flowing river, he began to notice the river. He saw abundant trees bearing all kinds of fruits on both sides of the river. The river brought life to swarms of living creatures wherever it flowed. Salt water turned into fresh water rejuvenating the surrounding areas. The Dead Sea was no longer "dead" but filled with all kinds of fish. Fishermen were happily casting their nets. The living creatures,

---

17. Ibid., 133.

River of Life

fruit trees, and the livelihood of the fishermen were sustained by the flow of the river that had its source in God, the Giver of Life.

The lesson from Ezekiel's vision is clear. Like the man in the vision, we too like to measure the depth of the river's flow in order to have things under our control.[18] We realize that this is not possible in our relationship with God. God, like the river, sets its own course and direction and we have no control over its flow. We need to yield to its ways in order to benefit from the flow of the river. We need to let the powerful flow of the river carry us along instead of crossing the river under our own strength. Prayer is essentially yielding to God's ways and meeting God on his terms. A matured prayer life that is yielded to God will abundantly bless and enrich others just like the trees and fishes that Ezekiel saw while sitting at the river's bank.

It is not easy to be carried by the flow of the river because we have no idea where the river will take us. The tranquility of the river may suddenly turn rough and stormy. The river may take us through some rough rapids where unseen dangers lurk below the surface. Some rivers in Malaysia are infested with man-eating crocodiles. Only the local folks know where these creatures are. Once we took a short mission trip to a remote village deep in the jungles of Sarawak, Malaysia. The village, Long Napir, was located by a river. We decided to take a boat ride to a nearby plantation one afternoon. It was an exciting ride as the boat sped through the rainforest. The trip by boat was uneventful until the river we were on flowed into a bigger river. We could feel the current getting stronger as the water suddenly swelled. We were holding tightly to our seats when things were getting rough for fear of getting drowned. The boat could easily flip over by the strong currents. Fortunately our guide was a skillful navigator who was familiar with the place. He was able to navigate his way out of the swelling waters with a long bamboo pole pushing against the riverbed. He could spot the dangerous places and avoid them because he knew where the deep and shallow waters were. Several times we needed to come down from the boat and walked a short distance,

---

18. Silf, *Landscapes of Prayer*, 52.

tripping our way over sharp rocks and sand, because the water was too shallow to navigate. The journey, filled with excitement and adventure, was risky.

Prayer is risky business. When we let God take over the reins of our life we never know where he is taking us. Life's rapids may just be around the corner and appear before us without much warning. God may lead us through tough times when we can feel the turbulence around us. Like the disciples in the midst of the stormy sea, we cry out to God for help. We wonder whether God really care if we are sucked in by the swelling waters. Occasionally, we need to disembark and walk a distance on dry land. These are the times when we feel that God has abandoned us when the rough sand and sharp rocks cause blisters on our feet. There are good times as well. The serenity and sounds of the rainforest give us delight and joy. We can feel the pulse of Mother Nature. Connected with nature, our hearts are free and at ease. Laughter fills the air and we behave like little kids with sheer delight and wonder. Awed by the mighty rainforest, we give praise and adoration to the wonder of God's creation.

Prayer is risky business only when we do not trust God to lead us. When we float on the water we need to trust its buoyancy to keep us afloat. To pray is to trust that God will watch over us and making sure that our foot will not slip while we struggle through life's journey. A story is told about a young boy whose house caught fire one night. He was forced to flee to the roof. The father, watching the fire slowly engulf the house, stood outside because he was not able to enter the house. The father, standing on the ground below the boy with outstretched arms, shouted, "Jump! I'll catch you." The boy had to jump to save his life. The boy couldn't see his father standing just below him. All he could see was thick smoke. He was afraid to jump though he heard clearly his father's voice. His father kept calling from below, "Jump! I will catch you." The boy protested, "Dad, I can't see you." The father replied, "But I can see you from here and that's all that matters." God can see though we may not see what is ahead of us. That is all that matters.

River of Life

VIEW FROM ABOVE

We finally reached our destination after more than ten hours of trekking over two mountain ranges and crossing two rivers. We were making our way to the first Baptist church in Saluron, Nepal. The church was planted by a local Nepali who received Christ when he was in Nagaland, India. He decided to come home to start his own ministry. There is a church now in every village on those mountains. The church was situated on a high mountain and we had a good view of the valley below. At this vantage point, we were able to see the various villages scattered across the mountain range. The river in the valley below was like a thread of silver gleaming under the rays of the hot sun. The roads zigzagged their way up and down the mountains. The roads looked tiny and the vehicles on them were like moving dots from a distance. I had no clue what kind of vehicles were on them, but my Nepali friends were able to distinguish a moving truck from a passenger bus. Things looked really different from this vantage point.

Having a right perspective is important because the way we perceive will shape our thinking and behavior. What we perceive to be true may not necessary be factual. Take for example the comparison between travelling by air and by land. We always think that land travel is safer because we are used to the idea that things fall from a height. The fact is that air travel is many times safer than land travel. Travelling in a plane at 35,000 feet sounds more dangerous than travelling on land by car. Besides, a plane accident is more catastrophic and damaging than a car accident. We feel more nervous, especially during takeoff and landing, in a plane than in a car even though flying is far safer than driving. We have perhaps seen too many graphic images of plane crashes or hijackings. They are played over and over on our television screens, which can make a dent on our emotional state of mind.

Philip Yancey, the best-selling evangelical author, stresses the need to view things from their source.[19] Most of us are not aware of the source of the river. In our prayers we start downstream and

19. Yancey, *Prayer*, 15–16.

bring our concerns and interests up to God. We tell God what we think he should do. We inform him of our woes and worries as if he has no clue at all about our current situation. We share with him our plan and expecting him to endorse it. We hardly want to see things from his perspective. We are more familiar with looking at things in the wrong direction. Our prayers are shaped and colored by the view from below, which is shaped and molded by clever advertising, fashion magazines, tabloid newspapers, cable television, social media, friends and neighbors, and many more. To correct this distorted vision, we need to put on the lens of prayer that views things from above, from God's perspective. We need to change direction by beginning upstream and starting at its source where the flow begins. Yancey writes:

> When I shift direction, I realize that God already cares about my concerns—my uncle's cancer, world peace, a broken family, a rebellious teenager—more than I do . . . I begin with God, who bears primary responsibility for what happens on earth, and ask what part I can play in God's work on earth.[20]

The psalmist, in Psalm 73, is envious of the wicked because they are prosperous. They seem to have no struggles and are in good health. Life has been good to them because they are not plagued by the burdens of life and suffer no mishaps. They have no fear of God in their hearts. They become proud and their speech testifies to their arrogance and confidence. People look up to their success and hope to emulate their good fortunes though their lifestyle is excessive and oppressive. Their wealth increases day by day and they live a carefree life. The psalmist frets when he compares himself with them. This fretfulness and envy affect his life before God and he is thinking of giving up on cultivating a pure heart before him. He says, "Surely in vain have I kept my heart pure; in vain have I washed my hands in innocence" (Ps 73:13).

The psalmist is in a fix because he views things from below and not from above. He needs to change direction. Instead of

20. Ibid., 15–16.

starting downstream, he needs to begin at its source where the flow begins. The psalmist is lamenting over the apparent prosperity and arrogance of the wicked for the first sixteen verses in Psalm 73. When he comes to verse seventeen, he changes perspective and sees things from God's point of view: "Till I entered the sanctuary of God; then I understand their final destiny." He now sees that the wicked are on slippery ground and all their wealth and good fortune will disappear like a dream. He then blames himself for behaving like a senseless, ignorant brute beast. He now changes his tune when he prays to God:

> Whom have I in heaven but you? And earth has nothing I desire besides you... But as for me, it is good to be near God. I have made the Sovereign Lord my refuge; I will tell of your deeds. (Ps 73:25, 28)

This change in perspective will change the way we pray. We now ask how we can work with God instead of asking him to work for us. We want to be partners with him and join him in his work to bless the world. God is always seeking our cooperation to be his co-partners. When he planted a garden in Eden, he called on Adam to tend it for him. He chose Moses to do the job for him when he wanted to make Israel a nation. He sought the help of David and later Solomon, along with thousands of workers, to build a temple for him. To become a human being, he needed the help of Mary to make it happen. He began by calling his disciples to follow him when he planned to build his church.

Conclusion

Prayer, like the river, is life-giving. Prayer is more than an act; it is a state of mind. It flows from our heart and mind to God unceasingly like the constant flow of a river. Anything can become prayer if we pay close attention to God in our daily life. To pray unceasingly is to be aware of God's presence in our life. Stopping time is one way for us to connect with God when we are too busy to pray. It is hard work because we need to maintain a sanctified relationship with

God, who calls us to be holy as he is holy. It is also risky because it is letting God take over the reins of our life and not knowing where he is leading us. Prayer begins with God, who is inviting us daily to join him in blessing the world. It is, therefore, needful to see the world from God's perspective. Prayer provides the lens for us to view things from above and not from below. We begin to grow in our prayer life as we trust God, yield to his ways, and meet him on his terms. Growth in prayer is growth in our relationship with God and others. Man is made to seek God and he can only find genuine joy and fulfillment only in him. That's all the more reason for us to pray.

QUESTIONS TO CONSIDER AND REFLECT

1. Why are Christians not as prayerful as they should be? Why is prayer hard work for many people?
2. Why is prayer so essential to the spiritual life? How do you know that you have matured in your prayer life?
3. Is it possible to pray unceasingly? Can you think of various ways you can do just that?
4. In what ways is your perspective of life informed by the view from below? How does prayer help you to correct this distortion and to view things from above, from God's perspective?

4

Sea of Turbulence

The human heart is like a ship on a stormy sea driven about by winds blowing from all four corners of heaven.

—Martin Luther

GOD'S POWER OVER THE SEA

I HAVE A GOOD view of the beach and sea from my balcony on the fourteenth floor. I get to know that the sea has her moods. On most days she is peaceful: a sea of calm with soothing shades of aqua marine. Watching the smooth sea with hardly a wave in sight brings a sense of stillness to my soul. Some days she has a playful mood: a sea of glittering gold caused by orange lights streaking through gaps in the clouds. The sight is awesome and I find my spirit soaring with her in celebration. At times she shows an angry face: dark clouds gathering on the horizon and strong winds turn the waters choppy. I can feel her fierce power in the wind. On rare occasions she shows her romantic side: a full moon beaming its lovely light on the silvery waves below. I look in silence while adoring the sacred moment. Once, her behavior took a sinister turn. When it hit us it was too late because no one expected it. There is a small cafe on the beach named Tsunami Village Cafe. The unusual name is a reminder that a tsunami had once hit the beach and nearly wiped out an entire fishing village. A massive tsunami caused by an earthquake in the Indian Ocean hit the northern beaches of Penang Island in Malaysia on December 26, 2004. The damage was minimal compared to the destruction in a neighboring country, where entire towns and villages were flattened and thousands of lives lost. Since then most of us who live near a beach in this part of the world have no doubt about the power of the sea.

The Bible often depicts the sea as chaotic, dangerous, and uncontrollable. The Israelites were never comfortable with the sea though they lived close to the Mediterranean Sea. The waters of the Red Sea that threatened to drown them, if not for the miraculous hand of God restraining the roaring waves, were an unforgettable experience. Israel had never been a sea-faring nation. Solomon had to depend on Hiram's ships to transport goods for the nation. The writer of Revelation, with a sigh of relief, announces that there will be no more sea in heaven. Israel's relationship with the sea is usually negative. The surging waters of the sea are usually compared to the experience of suffering, pain, and struggle. Overwhelmed by the surging waters of the raging sea, the psalmist writes, "All your waves and breakers have swept over me" (Ps 42:7). The psalmist, on the other hand, comes to know the sovereign power of God through the raging power of the sea. Only God can tame the mighty sea: "But at your rebuke the waters fled, at the sound of your thunder they took to flight . . . You set a boundary they cannot cross; never again will they cover the earth" (Ps 104:7, 9).

The walking on water and the stilling of the stormy sea by Jesus are prime examples of God's power over the sea. No man had done that before. The disciples were astounded and couldn't believe their eyes. "Who is this? He commands even the winds and the water, and they obey him" (Luke 8: 25). The disciples were reminded of the crossing of the Red Sea. The story of the miraculous

Sea of Turbulence

deliverance and salvation of God to save Israel from a watery death was known to all Israelites. Jesus' power over the sea shows that he also has power over life and death. He is able to deliver us from a sticky situation that is caused either by our fault or the result of our obedience to him. We are familiar with two sea stories in the Bible. The story of Jonah in the Old Testament and Paul's shipwreck in the New Testament are stories with similar plots. Both experience the peril of death by drowning at sea. Jonah is on a trip to avoid going to Nineveh out of disobeying God's call, while Paul is on a trip to Rome to face charges because of his obedience to the gospel. Both stories end with God saving them from the watery death so that they can be of service to him. Eugene Peterson has this to comment:

> Storm is the environment in which we either lose our lives or are saved; there is no cool, safe ledge on which to perch as spectators. There are no bleachers from which to enjoy the lightning and thunder, the waves and breakers of the storm. We are in it, prophet and people, sailors and saints. Nothing else matters at this point; it is life or death.[1]

WATERS OF AFFLICTION

Every Christian who is serious about his or her spiritual life must be a sailor at heart. We cannot stay on the beach and expect to work out our salvation with fear and trembling. Jesus calls us to move away from the shore and into deep waters. We need to stay at sea and experience its power in order to survive spiritually. Facing the storms of life is essential to our spiritual growth. We need the environment of the sea in order to experience the power of God at work in our life. God's preferred way of saving Israel was leading her through dangerous waters. God could have led her through a safer route but he didn't. It was through crossing the Red Sea that Israel came to know God's power over all the gods of Egypt. Israel

---

1. Peterson, *Under the Unpredictable Plant*, 68.

needed strong faith in order to survive in the Promised Land that was infested with idols just like Egypt. The Red Sea episode was a testimony to Israel that her God, though invisible, was more powerful than all the gods of Canaan. The psalmist writes:

> Yet he saved them for his name's sake, to make his mighty power known. He rebuked the Red Sea, and it dried up; he led them through the depths as through a desert. He saved them from the hand of the foe; from the hand of the enemy he redeemed them. The waters covered their adversaries; not one of them survived. Then they believed in his promises and sang his praise. (Ps 106:8–12)

God too charted a watery course for Jesus as he navigated his way through his earthly life. He was born in Bethlehem as a weak and helpless babe under threat from Herod's sword. He escaped to Egypt as a refugee in a foreign land. He could not go back to his own village upon his return but had to stay elsewhere for fear that his enemies would continue to seek him. He knew that he was moving into a trap when he decided to head toward Jerusalem. He would be accused, charged, and sentenced to death there. He faced the agony of impending death at Gethsemane. He prayed earnestly because he could feel the waves and breakers sweeping over him. Darkness, like the deep waters, overshadowed him at Golgotha. The darkness of sin separated him from his loving Father, who abandoned him at the point when he needed him the most. The darkness of Good Friday eventually led to the morning light of Easter dawn.[2]

God charts a watery course for us because he wants to use the disordered world to bring order to our life. Many of us are not aware of how disordered our life is. Our life, like the sea, is restless and lacks stability. Our uncontrolled desires are like the tossing waves of the sea. Life, on the surface, seems orderly and well managed until a storm hits us. "Trouble, at least extreme trouble," writes Peterson, "strips us to the essentials and reveals the basic reality of our lives."[3] One of the things that we notice when a tsunami hits

2. Mogabgab, "Editor's Introduction," 2–3.
3. Peterson, *Under the Unpredictable Plant*, 71.

Sea of Turbulence

the coast is the amount of debris it brings to the area. The hidden debris in our life begins to float to the surface. The waves cast up mire and mud (Isa 57:20). The raging storm discloses our human weakness and exposes our hidden faults. We begin to realize how fragile and helpless we are in the face of the stormy sea. Like the psalmist we cry out for salvation:

> Save me, O God, for the waters have come up to my neck.
> I sink in the miry depths where there is no foothold. I have come to the deep waters; the floods engulf me . . . Rescue me from the mire, do not let me sin." (Ps 69:1–2; 14)

God brings order out of chaos. The primordial chaos in the story of creation yielded to a word from God and the earth began to take shape. Light separated the darkness into day and night. The firmament separated the sky from the sea. The sea further separated into land and water. The land produced vegetation of various kinds. Now the creation was ready to welcome its inhabitants: sun, moon, stars, animals, birds, fishes, and finally human beings. Likewise, the storms that the disciples faced at Lake Galilee yielded to the word of Jesus: the sea turned calm. When chaos hits us, we call out to God to bring order to our life. This gives an opportunity for God's tough love to do the work of salvation in our souls.

The Puritans of the seventeenth century believed that afflictions were used by God to tame the heart. To Richard Baxter, a famous Puritan pastor, the heart is like "an untamed colt not used to the hand."[4] The Puritans were farmers who were tied to the soil. Being farmers, they were able to discern God's disciplinary hand in the natural world around them. Living in an enchanted world, they were filled with awe and wonder at the creation of God. They were, at the same time, terrified by the disturbances of the natural forces around them. To them, the inner chaos associated with the spiritual life was like the raging sea. Weathering the storms of life was a prelude to a purified desire for God. They took seriously Paul's words saying that Christians must go through many hard-

---

4. Baxter, *The Saints' Everlasting Rest*, 147.

ships to enter the kingdom of God (Acts 14:22). Hardships were occasions used by God to cleanse their soul, purify their faith, and strengthen their relationship with him. Their uncontrolled passions were now curbed and channeled to good use. They were able to unbridle their affections and to wean them from the temporal things of life.

Anne Bradstreet compared God's use of affliction to a mother's weaning her baby by rubbing wormwood or mustard on her breast. Knowing how easily she could fall in love with the world and be dependent on it for earthly joys, she lamented saying, "I have found by experience, I can no more live without correction than without food."[5] She took delight in difficulties because every affliction that brought chaos to her life revealed God's love and power that could wean her from earthly attachments. Samuel Rutherford, a Scottish theologian and author, shared the same sentiment. He said, "When I am in the cellar of affliction, I look for the Lord's choicest wines."[6]

FEAR OF DEATH

We tend to respond with terror when faced with the waters of affliction. The disciples of Jesus were terrified when faced with stormy weather at sea because of the fear of drowning. Jesus, meanwhile, was fast asleep at the stern of the boat. Apparently he was oblivious to the raging storm around him. In this scene we see two contrasting pictures: Jesus' complete trust in God's protection and care, and the disciples' lack of trust revealed in their fear for their lives. The fear of death at sea is very real. No wonder we view the sea as a "watery grave." Jonah feared for his life when he was cast into the sea by the sailors: "You hurled me into the deep, into the very heart of the seas . . . from the depths of the grave I called for help, and you listened to my cry" (Jon 2:3, 2).

---

5. Backstreet, *The Works of Anne Backstreet*, 38, quoted in Lane, *Ravished by Beauty*, 145.

6. Lane, *Ravished by Beauty*, 146.

Sea of Turbulence

Many years ago I took an interest in the rehab work of drug addicts. In those days Hong Kong was a notorious place for drug abuse. I went there to study and to know more about working with hardcore drug addicts. I was taken to a remote island that served as a rehab center for drug addicts. Supplies were transported by boat from Kowloon to the deserted island once a week. The weekly supplies were basic stuff like sugar, rice, salt, and oil. The addicts had to plant their own vegetables and catch fish from the sea. Our daily diet was simple: plain noodles flavored with chili oil for breakfast and lunch, fresh fish and steaming rice for dinner. I always looked forward to the evening meal because the fresh fish caught from the sea when steamed with chili oil had an excellent taste and texture. Once I was asked to jump into the sea below when the boat was in deep water. The boys, who were all good swimmers, wanted to test my courage. I told them I was not a swimmer but they insisted. They assured me that they would rescue me if I would sink to the bottom. I held my breath and jumped into the cold dark waters trying to grab the side of the boat the moment I surfaced. Fortunately they had the life buoy ready for me in case I needed it. The experience was unforgettable and terrifying.

Our greatest fear is the fear of death. We avoid the issue of death by devising all kinds of coping measures to deny our mortality though we know that death is imminent. We cannot avoid it because we are reminded of it whenever we watch the news or read the papers or hear that someone we know has passed away. The greatest impact will be when someone whom we love passes away. We often think that death can happen to someone else and not to us or our loved ones. We tend to think that death is separated from life. Death, in fact, is the end of life and a part of life's rhythm. Mark Twain once remarked that only those who have lived fully are most prepared to die. Conversely, those who are ready to face death will learn to value and live life to its fullest potential. Alan Jones in his book *Soul Making* writes:

> The more we refuse to look at our own death, the more we repress and deny new possibilities for living. We are all going to die, and our life is a movement to that sure

end. Believers find that meditation on this simple fact has a wonderful way of clearing the mind! It enables them to live every single moment with new appreciation and delight. When I say to myself, "This moment may be my last," I am able to see the world with new eyes.[7]

My wife was diagnosed with ovarian cancer many years ago. Her life changed drastically since that encounter with death. She lived life to the full. Shortly after this incident, she initiated a Bible study group for women in the city that led to hundreds attending the weekly classes. Nouwen wrote that death is a gift: "Death can be made into a final gift if we have lived carefully and gracefully."[8] He further wrote that only the beloved of God can welcome death as a gift instead of fearing it.[9]

As God's beloved we should not be enslaved by the fear of death. Jesus died to "free those who all their lives were held in slavery by the fear of death" (Heb 2:15). Christ, through his resurrection, has broken the power of sin and death over us. We can now face death positively and this ought to change the way we think and live. With our greatest fear put aside by the cross, we should be able to deal with the many "deaths" that we experience throughout our life. Every loss we face in life causes us to die a little. Life is a series of losses. We lose the warm and security of the womb the moment we are born into this world. We lose the protection of home when we attend school for the first time. When we get married, we lose the freedom of singlehood. When we have children, we lose sleep taking care of them. We lose our economic freedom after we retire. We lose our hair and teeth when we grow old. When we die, we lose everything. We should not be afraid of these losses. Faith in the resurrected Christ will overcome our fear of loss and death.

John Bunyan was a non-conformist writer and preacher of seventeenth-century England. His book, *The Pilgrim's Progress*, gives an account of the fears a Christian pilgrim faces when he lives out his faith in a hostile world. One day Mr. Great-Heart came

7. Jones, *Soul Making*, 67.
8. Nouwen, *Creative Ministry*, 47.
9. Nouwen, *Our Greatest Gift*, 25.

across some lions that hindered his journey to the Celestial City. Mr. Great-Heart, with sword in hand, was not afraid and ready to face the lions. The others that went with him were happy to lag behind out of fear. The path, overgrown with grass, was not used by many pilgrims. Most avoided this path because of the lions. Mr. Great-Heart noticed that these fierce lions were chained as he was going forward to them. Their freedom to cause harm was limited, and the most they could cause fear to the pilgrims was their roar. The allegory points out that the enemies of our faith will always be there to haunt and frighten us. They can only roar but not devour. Someone who has gone before us has neutralized their power to harm and cause damage to our faith. We should not be afraid of the waves and breakers of the sea no matter how frightening is the roar. The children in Sunday school love to sing this song: "With Christ in the vessel we can smile at the storm." This is echoed by the prophet Isaiah in his words to the returning exiles from Babylon: "When you pass through the waters, I will be with you; and when you pass through the rivers, they will not sweep over you" (Isa 43:2).

THE GIFT OF WONDER

The sea is as mysterious as it is unpredictable. We can only see the sea's surface while standing at the edge of the sea. The secret life of the sea lies in the deep, and what lurks beneath is inscrutable and unfathomable. The vastness and irresistible power of the sea, like its Creator, is a mystery to us. Its many moods, ranging from anger to playfulness, cause us to marvel and wonder. The psalmist, filled with wonder at the mystery of the sea, exclaims, "How many are your works, O Lord! There is the sea, vast and spacious, teeming with creatures beyond number—living things both large and small" (Ps 104:24–25). The sea, teeming with all kinds of sea creatures, is a source of livelihood for many people. Jesus called on the disciples to cast their net on the right side as he prepared breakfast with their catch. They hesitated because they worked all night and caught nothing. They then decided to take Jesus' advice to cast their net one more time. The catch was so plentiful that it broke the net. Discouragement led to joy and wonder.

The sea reminds us of the mystery and wonder of nature that is around us. Our human spirit thrives on wonder and mystery. According to Albert Einstein, the most beautiful experience is mysterious. Without it we are "as good as dead and our eyes are diminished."[10] It is unfortunate that our capacity to wonder has diminished when replaced by rationality. Disenchantment of our world took place with the advent of science and technology. In the modern world, science seeks answers from nature and technology uses these answers to master nature for our own advancement and progress. The gift of wonder calls us back to see the world as mysterious and sacred. There are two ways to know and respond to the world around us: the way of reason and the way of wonder.[11] Reason seeks to tame, exploit, and to have control whereas wonder responds to the mysteries of life around us without attempting to impose by seeking for answers. Wonder requires us to be open and attentive to the things around us. With wonder the ordinary things can become extraordinary when they receive our attention.[12] Unlike children who are gifted with wonder, adults find it hard to view life with awe and reverence. Our busy lifestyle does not permit us to slow down, pause, and see things as they are. Wonder does not impose on its object but let it speak with its own voice.

Esther de Waal is a writer of Benedictine and Celtic spirituality. In her book *Lost in Wonder* she relates how Thomas Merton used his camera to capture the world around him. At first his journalist friend, John Howard Griffin, was puzzled when he received the photos from Merton. He knew from the photographs that Merton viewed things differently from most people. Most people would not take photos of an old fence or shack, weeds growing between cracks, working gloves on a stool, a dead root, or a broken

---

10. Einstein, *Ideas and Opinions*, 11, quoted in Benner, *Soulful Spirituality*, 109.

11. Heschel, *Man Is Not Alone*, 13, quoted in Benner, *Soulful Spirituality*, 111.

12. Benner, *Soulful Spirituality*, 114.

Sea of Turbulence

stone wall. Merton was not searching for something to photograph but to use his camera on whatever crossed his path. He gave each item his attention but never imposed on them. Instead he allowed each thing to speak on its own terms and to have its own voice.[13] Once Merton reprimanded a fellow photographer for the way he approached things with his camera. He told him to stop looking and to begin seeing:

> Because looking means that you have something in mind for your eye to find; you've set out in search of your desired object and have closed off everything else presenting itself along the way. But seeing is being open and receptive to what comes to the eye; your vision total and not targeted.[14]

Today I met a student when I was on my way to the library. I noticed some cute, colorful moths fluttering among the bushes while talking to him. I noticed them while talking to the student though I did not look out for them. My eyes were being open and receptive to whatever crossed my path. They were just ordinary moths. They became extraordinary because I allowed them to speak on their own terms and have their own voice. I turned to my student and said, "Look at the moths; aren't they lovely?" Everything around us can take on a sacred quality and become a prayer when we take time and space in our tight schedule to look at them with childlike curiosity and awe.

What led Adam and Eve to sin in the garden of Eden? Was it the lack of awe and wonder?[15] I am sure Adam and Eve enjoyed their time and fellowship with God in the garden surrounded by trees pleasing to the eyes and fruit good for food. Filled with a sense of wonder and awe at God's creation, their lives were carefree and at ease. One day something changed. Their eyes were now set on a desired object instead of seeing things that crossed their path with wonder. They took an interest in a particular tree: the tree

---

13. Waal, *Lost in Wonder*, 64.
14. Seitz, *Song for Nobody*, 133–34, quoted in Waal, *Lost in Wonder*, 64.
15. Waal, *Lost in Wonder*, 56.

of the knowledge of good and evil. They now spent time looking out for the one tree in the garden that would make them wise at the urging of the old serpent. They wanted to own and have control over this tree and wanted its fruit. The fall to sin led them to lose their primitive wonder and childlike awe. Reason took over with this new knowledge. They saw their own nakedness and were ashamed of what they saw and made fig leaves to cover themselves. Their relationship with nature and God changed drastically. They figured that God would not be happy seeing their shame and they hid from him.

ADRIFT AND RESTLESS

Our life, like the restless sea, is constantly in flux. Carried by the wind and waves, we have no idea where these will take us. We look forward to solid ground and a place to land and sink our roots when adrift. Noah was adrift and he watched for days looking out for a safe place to land after the violence of the deluge. Paul and the sailors were adrift, during a severe storm, for many days in the ocean hoping to see land. The disciples were adrift when they saw their master suffered a violent death at the cross. Discouraged and disorientated by the sudden events, they huddled among themselves in a room wondering what would happen next. When adrift we tend to ask what will happen next and what shall we do next.[16] Being adrift is a modern phenomenon. Not rooted or grounded to a center, modern people tend to live for the future and accept change as a permanent feature of their lives. Change, like the constant flux of the sea, is the norm rather than the exception. Perhaps this is why life in a mobile society appears to be shallow and superficial. Rootedness, according to Simone Weil, is the most important and least recognized need of the human soul.[17] Thomas Kelly, a Quaker and author of the spiritual classic *A Testament of Devotion*, has this to say:

16. Doughty, "Adrift," 2, 18.
17. Weil, *The Need for Roots*, 3.

> We are not skilled in the inner life where the real roots of our problem lie ... the outer distractions of our interests reflects an inner lack of integration of our own selves. We are trying to be several selves at once, without all our selves being organized by a single, mastering Life within us.[18]

We feel adrift and anchorless in the modern world when swarmed by myriads of activities that threaten to drown us. Lacking inner integration, we lose our bearings in the midst of busyness. We are adrift in the world of activism and overwork. Merton calls this a form of contemporary violence that is pervasive in the modern world:

> The rush and pressure of modern life are a form, perhaps the most common form, of its innate violence. To allow oneself to be carried away by a multitude of conflicting concerns, to surrender to too many demands, to commit oneself to too many projects, to want to help everyone in everything, is to succumb to violence ... It kills the root of inner wisdom which makes work fruitful.[19]

We need an anchor or a rope to keep us grounded and to prevent us from drifting. Parker Palmer, in his book *A Hidden Wholeness*, relates a story about some farmers who would tie a rope from the back door of their house to the barn during a blizzard. This was to ensure that they would return home safely after a trip outside the house. Severe blizzards could be dangerous and could cause visibility problems. The farmers wandered in circles in their own backyards unable to see properly during a heavy snowstorm. Some were frozen to death when exposed to such cold weather. The rope in their hands was the only way to guide them back to their house. They needed to hold on to it tightly to find their way home.[20] It was their lifeline.

Disoriented by the constant flux of life, we need to reorient ourselves to our home: a place centered and rooted in God. To

---

18. Kelly, *A Testament of Devotion*, 91.
19. Quoted in Scazerro, *Emotionally Healthy Spirituality*, 173.
20. Ibid., 153.

Peter Scazzero, Sabbath keeping is "the rope that leads us back to God in the blizzards of life. It acts as our anchor for living in the hurricane of demands."[21] Sabbath sets the weekly rhythm for us to find our bearings again after six busy days of work. After creating the world, God established the weekly rhythm of six days of work and a day set aside for rest, worship, and prayer. He set an example for us by resting on the seventh day and he mandated that his people followed this divine rhythm also. The most specific and longest of all the Ten Commandments is the fourth commandment (four out of the fifteen verses), to remember the Sabbath and keep it holy:

> Remember the Sabbath by keeping it holy. Six days you shall labor and do all your work, but the seventh day is a Sabbath to the Lord your God. On it you shall not do any work, neither you, nor your son or daughter, nor your manservant or maidservant, nor your animals, nor the alien within your gates. For in six days the Lord made the heavens and the earth, the sea, and all that is in them, but he rested on the seventh day. Therefore the Lord blessed the Sabbath day and made it holy. (Exod 20:8-11)

RHYTHMS OF LIFE

Rhythm is essential to life, spiritually and physically. We are to live in sync with the rhythmic nature of the world because rhythm is built in our bodies and embedded in our world. The waves hit the shore, one after another, at regular intervals. Like the waves, we breathe in and out with rhythmic fashion. We cannot exhale unless we first inhale air into our lungs. Day and night influence the way we live and our daily activities are in rhythm with the rising and setting of the sun. There is a rhythmic structure in the creation account. Each day begins and ends with, "And God said . . . And there was evening and there was morning." The same sequence is repeated six times for the first six days. On the seventh day, the

---

21. Ibid., 155.

sequence is broken, for it is not like the first six days. They are like "a kind of symphony in six moments."[22] Peterson claims that if we read the text in the creation account, it "gets inside us. We enter the rhythms of creation time and find that we are internalizing a creation sense of orderliness and connectedness and resonance that is very much like what we get from music."[23]

We love listening to music but hate noise because music rhythms with time whereas noise is erratic and is a dissonance with time. Noise has a negative effect on our behavior because noise pollution is bad for our physiological and psychological health. It leads the list of environmental stressors.[24] Studies have shown that a quiet ambience increases the efficiency of workers. Conversely, those who have been exposed to noise tend to make more errors and get more frustrated in their work. Psychologist Sheldon Cohen made this discovery in a classic study of the chronic environmental impact of overstimulation on children. A study was made on the impact of traffic noise on children who lived in an apartment on a busy New York street. The study showed that children who lived on the lower floors and were subjected to more noise pollution had reading and hearing skills worse than those living on higher floors.[25]

The same goes with hurry, which is a prevalent feature of modern living. Like Merton, Peterson thinks that hurry is a "form of violence practiced on time."[26] Time is God's gift to us but hurry does violence to this gift by desecrating it. Time is no longer seen as a gift but a commodity that we can use and manage. We hurry because we want to keep time with work and other forms of activities that need our attention. Sabbath is good for our soul because it protects us from being swamped by the tyranny of hurried time. Sabbath stops us on our tracks and gives us time to pause and

22. Sittser, *Water from a Deep Well*, 99.
23. Peterson, *Christ Plays in Ten Thousand Places*, 67.
24. Gallagher, *The Power of Place*, 153–54.
25. Cohen, *Journal of Experimental Social Psychology*, 1973, quoted in Gallagher, *The Power of Place*, 158.
26. Peterson, *Answering God*, 61.

reflect on our work in this world. It reminds us that our work is an extension of God's work in his created world. We are his hands and legs to serve the common good. Our work, without God in it, is a liability and snare to our soul. It becomes an idol that slowly but surely suffocates our spiritual life.

Conclusion

Only God can tame the sea. God's preferred way of dealing with us is to lead us through dangerous waters where we can witness the power of God at work in our life. The storms of life, in the form of hardships and difficulties, are used by God to bring order and growth to our soul. The sea threatens our existence and we often associate it with death. God's power over sin and death at the cross should help us overcome this fear of death. The sea, like God, is mysterious and unpredictable. We sense the wonder around us by looking at the sea. We need the gift of wonder in order to live fully, for our human spirit thrives on wonder and mystery. Our life, like the sea, is in a state of flux and turbulence. Adrift and restless, we look for solid ground to land. Hurry, filled with activism and overwork, disorientates and causes dissonance to the rhythm of life. Sabbath keeping sets the rhythm of our life because it centers our life on God and not on the self. Like an anchor to our soul, it stops us from being adrift in the turbulent sea.

QUESTIONS TO CONSIDER AND REFLECT

1. What is your response to the afflictions in your life? Do you think that afflictions can be used to show God's power?
2. Why do most people fear death and avoid it like a plague? Can a more positive view of death help us to live better?
3. Adults find it hard to view life with reverence and awe. Why are we not gifted with a sense of wonder like little children?

Are there ways for us to regain this sense of wonder in our life?

4. Explain why being adrift and restless is a modern phenomenon. How has this modern phenomenon impact your spiritual life? How should you address this problem?

5

Desert of Transformation

A person is forced inward by the sparseness of what is outward and visible in all this land and sky. The beauty of the Plains is like that of an icon . . . what seems stern and almost empty is merely open, a door into some simple and holy state.

—Kathleen Norris[1]

THE CALL OF THE DESERT

THE DESERT IS MARKED by extremes: hot during the day and cold at night. It is a barren, empty landscape with endless sand and rock. The rainfall is less than ten inches per annum, and in some places the rain evaporates before it reaches the ground. The rate of evaporation exceeds the rate of precipitation in the desert. The temperature at ground level can be so intense that the wind at such heat can cause a human being to dehydrate rapidly. The place is not fit for human habitation because there are no provisions and

---

1. Norris, *Dakota*, 157.

Desert of Transformation

conveniences available for decent living. Yet the solitary desert, filled with emptiness and dangerous wildlife, is the ideal place for people who seek a solitary life. Undistracted and stripped of worldly possessions and pleasure, they are able to pursue their life with God in solitude and silence. It is the ideal place to grow the spiritual life.

The desert fathers, during the fourth and fifth centuries, fled to the desert to seek God and to deal with the compulsions of life. They turned their backs from the world, the flesh, and the devil in order to live a life in total surrender to God. Life was simple in the desert: a cave or a stone hut with a roof of branches over it, a mat for a bed, a sheepskin to keep warm, a jar of water to quench thirst, and a lamp to give light. Sleep was kept to a minimum and a meal a day was the norm. Their daily diet consisted of dry bread, water, salt, some oil, and vegetables. They followed a rhythm of work and prayer. They weaved mats and baskets to support their daily living. This simple, uncluttered life helped them to be attentive in seeking after God. Solitude and silence set the conditions necessary for prayer. This did not mean that there were no temptations in the desert. The worldly temptations they left behind had now turned inward. The world within their hearts was even harder to deal with than the outside world. The greatest fear of the desert fathers and mothers was not the world they left behind but the world they carried within them. Abba Anthony once said:

> The man, who abides in solitude and is quiet, is delivered from fighting three battles—those of hearing, speech, and sight. Then he will have but one battle to fight—the battle of the heart.[2]

The desert has been the preferred place to train God's servants. It is an ideal place of transformation because the ruggedness of the place calls for a rugged faith in its inhabitants. The Bible has plenty of examples of men and women with rugged faith trained by the desert landscape. Abraham, a man of the city, received a call to leave for the desert country of Canaan. Moses spent forty years

2. Chadwick, *Western Asceticism*, 40.

in the desert tending sheep. David spent time in the desert fleeing from Saul, who wanted to end his life. John the Baptist appeared on the scene as a desert preacher with a message of repentance. Paul spent some years in the wilderness of Arabia before he could be an apostle to the Gentiles. Jesus was not spared of the desert as a training ground. He was driven by the Spirit to be tempted by the devil in the desert after his baptism. Jesus often retreated to a solitary place to be alone with God throughout his ministry. The wilderness mentioned in the Bible is a semi-arid place—not a true desert like the Sahara or Sinai. The wilderness, like the true desert, is a tough place for daily existence because it lacks human habitation and resources for living. The wilderness provides the opportunity for a person to spend time with God unhindered by people and other distractions. To be alone in solitude with God is the desert's gift to us.[3]

The solitary life, if misunderstood, can lead to excesses. Desert training is a means to wean oneself from the temptations of the flesh. The goal is to master one's carnal desires. The real enemy is the darkness that resides in the heart. The disciplines, if misguided, can lead some people to become proud of their feats. This causes more harm than good to the soul.[4] One day three zealous monks visited an old monk. The first proudly proclaimed that he could recite the entire Bible from memory. "You have filled the air with words," the old man replied. The next person claimed that he had copied by hand the whole Bible. "You have managed to line your book shelf with a few more books," the old man warned. The last person confided that his chimney had grass growing in it, meaning that he had not used fire to heat his place even during winter. The old man remarked, "You have driven away hospitality."[5]

The true solitary life calls for moderation instead of excesses. A young man came to Abba Silvanus to complain about certain monks who were wasting time doing common chores instead of spending time praying. He used the example of Mary in the

---

3. See Rensberger, "Deserted Spaces," 7.
4. Sittser, *Water from a Deep Well*, 89.
5. Chadwick, *Western Asceticism*, 126.

Desert of Transformation

Bible to support his point. He quoted Jesus saying that Mary had chosen the better part compared with busy Martha. Abba Silvanus ordered for the young man to be put in a cell and given a book to read. He wondered why no one had brought him food when it was time for the evening meal. He found Abba Silvanus and asked whether the monks had eaten. He replied that they indeed had eaten. The young man asked why he was not called to the table. Silvanus replied, "You are a spiritual person and do not need food. We have to work with our hands since we are carnal and want to eat. But you have chosen the better part and read all day without the need for food." The young man understood the Abba's words and repented of his lack of discernment. "Forgive me, Abba," he said. The old man said to him, "Mary needs Martha. It is really thanks to Martha that Mary is praised."[6]

THE BATTLE OF THE SOUL

The biography of Antony of Egypt written by Athanasius, bishop of Alexandria in the fourth century AD, helped the spread of the monastic movement. It was later translated into Latin by Evagrius of Antioch. It became one of the best-known works in the Christian world at that time. Anthony is often called the father of monasticism and a leader of the desert fathers. Athanasius wrote about the supernatural temptations that Anthony faced in the desert in the biography. He fought with demons while living in a cave. At first the devil assaulted his mind with a barrage of unsettling thoughts: flattery, worldly pleasures, fleshy lust, vocational sacrifices, and many more. Undeterred by such temptations, he devoted himself in vigilant prayers, fasting, and ascetic labors. The devil decided to attack Anthony physically after having failed in his mental assault. A gang of demons came one night to attack the monk until he nearly died. Bruised and unable to stand, Anthony cried out in a loud voice challenging the demons to continue with their assault. He reminded them that they would not be able to separate him

---

6. Ward, *The Sayings of the Desert Fathers*, 223.

from his beloved Christ. He encouraged himself by singing the Psalms. The subsequent attacks became more fierce and threatening. The wall of the cave shook and the demons appeared in the forms of wild beasts. Snakes, lions, wolves, and bulls appeared to assault and frighten Anthony. He quickly recognized the enemy's impotence and was not afraid. They could roar or hiss, but they could not hurt him, for the Lord was his shield and wall of safety.

In the desert the most likely demons we do battle with are our own. The battle of our heart or soul is the fight that each of us has to face. We are vulnerable to temptation and fall into sin because of the thoughts that afflict our minds. Evagrius identified eight of these deadly thoughts: gluttony, lust, greed, sadness, anger, sloth, vainglory, and pride. It is pride that is viewed as the beginning of the seven deadly sins. Jesus was tempted by Satan three times in the wilderness. Each time the words of Satan appealed to Jesus' pride and inner voice. The first temptation was to change stone into bread because Satan knew that Jesus was hungry. Jesus had the power to satisfy his hunger as God's Son. But he resisted by saying, "Man does not live on bread alone." Then he was tempted the second time. He was taken to a high place and shown all the kingdoms of the world. Satan promised to give him all these kingdoms, along with their authority and splendor, if he would bow down to him in worship. This appealed to his pride. He could have the crown without the cross of humiliation. Again Jesus resisted by saying, "Worship the Lord your God and serve him only." Then he was asked to jump from a high tower. Jesus knew that he had the power to call his angels to help him land safely. He again resisted the temptation and said, "Do not put the Lord your God to the test." If Jesus listened to his pride and inner voice he would have failed, but he resisted by listening to God instead.

The most formidable enemy lies within us. It is the homemade self that we have nurtured from young. At a young age we instinctively conceived this idea that we can only be happy if our fundamental needs are met satisfactorily. The needs of security and survival, esteem and affection, power and control will lead to

Desert of Transformation

the formation of the false self.[7] The self is king and any outside stimulus that threatens our sense of security and survival, esteem and affection, power and control will be rejected. Conversely, any stimulus that enhances these fundamental needs will be welcomed. It is not surprising that these deadly thoughts identified by Evagrius appeal to our strong sense of self and can cause us to be tempted and fall into sin. The false self listens to its own voice rather than the voice of God. We must learn to vacate the false self in us and make space for God in our heart.

THE SELF MUST DIE

The call of the desert is a call to emptiness. The desert is scarce on many things but not on empty space. Unlike the city or forest, a person can see a great distance in a desert. Sue Monk Kidd, in her book *God's Joyful Surprise*, calls us to consider the spaces that God has designed in the world.[8] The spaces between trees give the forest its serenity. There will be no music if there are no spaces between the notes of a concerto or symphony. Words become meaningful when there are spaces between them. She recalls the time when her daughter Ann was playing with the typewriter. She kept hitting the keys without touching the space bar. The words all ran together that didn't make sense. Our life is just like that. We hardly hit the space bar. We need to make space for God and the way to do it is to empty ourselves. We need to empty ourselves of the false self in order for the true self to be resurrected. When Jesus spoke of his death he reminded his audience about a kernel of wheat falling to the ground. If it doesn't die it will remain a single seed; if it dies it will produce many more seeds. New life springs up when death occurs. One way to empty ourselves is the abandonment of control. The desert has a clever way in doing that. The silence and solitude one encounters in the desert will lead to the abandonment of self.

---

7. Keating, *The Human Condition*, 13–14.
8. Kidd, *God's Joyful Surprise*, 161–62.

The first thing we learn in the abandonment of self is to die to speech. Julian of Norwich suddenly became ill for three days when she was thirty years old. She lost her ability to speak and her sight slowly failed her. She was given up as dead and the last rites were administered to her. During this time when she was in utter silence and losing control of her life, she went through an extraordinary experience that would impact her for the rest of her life. Later she would teach about poverty of self made aware by the utter impotence in silent prayer. Language is often used as an agent of control. We use words to manipulate, influence, and propagate. No wonder silence is painful and unbearable to many of us.[9] Stephen Kurtz, looking from a psychoanalyst's point of view, writes:

> In renouncing speech . . . we yield up something fundamentally human—a central means for declaring and expressing our existence. It is a kind of annihilation. Viewed this way, silence is equated to death. To discover that our lives are "rooted in silence that is not death but life" one must first keep quiet.[10]

We not only die to speech but we also die to self in the desert. The desert ignores our presence totally. To Edward Abbey, author and radical environmentalist, this is the desert's gift to us:

> The fine quality of these stones, these plants and animals, this desert landscape is the indifference manifest to our presence, our absence, our coming, our staying or our going. Whether we live or die, is a matter of absolute no concern whatsoever to the desert.[11]

Like Job, our world may come crashing down and falling into pieces. We feel the pain and cry out in bitterness to God. Yet God, like the desert, is indifferent to our pain. We feel emptiness inside us when our life is being stripped away. This nothingness reflects the empty spaces of the desert. Out of nothingness, the self

---

9. Mah, *Being Truly Human*, 30–31.
10. Kurtz, "Silence" 137.
11. Abbey, *Desert Solitaire*, 267.

Desert of Transformation

abandons itself to God. Meister Eckhart, German theologian and mystic, has this to say about abandonment:

> If you want to live and want your works to live, you must be dead to all things, and have become nothing. It is characteristic of creatures that they make something out of something, while it is characteristic of God that he makes something out of nothing. Therefore, if God is to make anything in you or with you, you must first have become nothing.[12]

The desert also trains us to die to our neighbor. We tend to view ourselves through the lens of others. The compulsive preoccupation with what others think of us means that we are dealing with a self-image that needs constant mending. The desert is indifferent to all this panting for attention. There is no gallery for the false self to play to; there is no audience. All is emptiness. We are free to be ourselves when there is no one to applaud or criticize us. We no longer care about how or what people think of us because we do not subject ourselves to the dictates of others. We are indeed free when we die to our neighbor.[13] Take the example of Abba Moses:

A magistrate in the city was keen to meet Abba Moses for he heard that he was a devout person. He came to the desert with the aim to search for him. He asked to see the father when he met the first person he came across. The man told the magistrate not to waste his time looking for the old monk for he would be disappointed. He quietly whispered to him that this Abba Moses was a fraud and a heretic. He was not what people said he was. He urged the magistrate not to search further but to return home. This new revelation deeply disappointed him. The magistrate returned home to his friends and relatives. He was keen to bring down the reputation of this monk before them. Then someone asked him to describe exactly the person he met in the desert. "Was he by chance a tall black man?" he asked. The magistrate replied in the

---

12. Eckhart, "German Sermon 39" 296–97.
13. Mah, *Being Truly Human*, 34.

affirmative. He was told that the man he met was indeed Abba Moses. The magistrate went away greatly edified.[14]

SOLITUDE AND SILENCE[15]

Most of us do not live in a desert. We can instead detour daily to a solitary place to pray in silence and solitude. One day a monk asked Abba Moses for a word of wisdom. "Go and sit in your cell and your cell will teach you everything," he told him.[16] The monk, when confined to a time of solitude and silence in the cell, would open a space in his heart for God to teach him the way of the desert. Sitting in solitude and silence has a way of wearing down our strong sense of self due to our attachment to things, people, and ideas. Blaise Pascal, French mathematician and Christian philosopher, once wrote that all the unhappiness of men arises from one single fact: that they cannot stay quietly in their own room.[17]

The practice of solitude and silence is a challenge for us who live in an age of hurry. We lack the patience to sit still in the cell for long. An inner world of chaos opens up in us the moment we shut the outer world of noise and people behind us. Shutting the door behind us does not mean that we have gotten rid of the world. We carry the world into our solitude and silence. We give up the practice easily when distracted by all these noises and thoughts in our head. We want to get busy again so that it will shield us from the inner chaos. It is difficult to be alone because the inner thoughts of feelings, fantasies, ideas, memories, and desires are like the wild beasts that keep assaulting us. They keep knocking at our mind's door and will not leave us alone. How to get rid of them? The trick is not to pay attention to them. We must not fight against these intruding thoughts and feelings. We acknowledge their existence and let them pass by. Suppose a familiar face passes by when I am

14. Ward, trans., *The Sayings of the Desert Fathers*, 140.
15. Material in this section is taken from my book *Being Truly Human*, 39, 43–47.
16. Ward, trans., *The Sayings of the Desert Fathers*, 139.
17. Pascal, *Pensees*, 42.

Desert of Transformation

in deep conversation with another person. I will acknowledge her presence with a nod and continue to talk to my friend. The knocking, after some time, will diminish if I do not open the door and let in the visitors. Unwelcomed, the visitors will slowly fade away. The knocking becomes less but it will not go away altogether. We can only reap its benefits if we persevere to stay put in the cell.

There is no one correct or best way to observe this discipline. Each person is different in temperament and personality and has to find her own niche. Nevertheless, for those who want to grow in this discipline, certain guidelines need to be observed. First of all, we must be committed to exercising this discipline on a regular basis. We will not reap any benefit out of it if we do it on an ad hoc or inconsistent basis. Rhythm and flow are critical to the progress of any spiritual discipline. We need to do it at least once a day. It is also essential that we practice this discipline in a familiar place and at a fixed time. Changing place and time often will disrupt the rhythm and flow needful for growth in the discipline.

The place must be free from all kinds of distractions. A room or space cluttered with things is not conducive because it reminds us of unfinished tasks that need our attention. If we do not have the luxury to afford an uncluttered space, we can do our solitude and silence early in the morning when the place is still dark. In this way, we will not notice the things around us. The place must be free from all sources of unwelcomed noises coming from the phone, radio, and television. God alone will have our attention in solitude and silence.

The place must be well ventilated with a good flow of fresh air so that we can stay alert. The air temperature is also important because too cold or too warm will bring physical discomfort. The spot chosen to settle down for the discipline must be comfortable but not too comfortable to the body. Sleep and drowsiness may be induced by too comfortable a spot. Any physical discomfort caused by the environment can be a distraction and a hindrance to the practice of solitude and silence. We may need to experiment with various spots in the house to get the optimal space for our discipline. We must try to stick to it as long as we can once we have decided on a spot.

Our posture should keep us alert at all times. We need to experiment with various postures and choose one that is optimal to the discipline. A posture that will keep us alert and not induce us to sleep or feel lazy is the right one. I find that kneeling with my back straight with a pillow underneath my legs will keep me comfortable and alert at the same time. We should also pay attention to our breathing. Deep, correct breathing will help the body to relax and the mind to be attentive.

How long should we spend in solitude and silence? We should begin in baby steps. A few minutes at the beginning is sufficient. As we progress, we can increase the time to about twenty minutes to half an hour a day. Time passes quickly when we get deeper into the practice of solitude and silence. It is good to end this time by saying the Lord's Prayer aloud. We may want to continue this time with verbalized prayers, praises, and petitions to God.

We should not have expectations during this time of silent prayer. To expect something is to orient our minds or thoughts to something else other than God. Our attention, or rather our intention, should be on God and not on our thoughts, feelings, or concepts. We should reach God with pure faith. It is not easy to let go of our thoughts to reach God with pure faith. Hence we need something to center ourselves. We need a prayer word to help us open to God and to his presence. The meaning of the prayer word is not important. The use of the prayer word is to express our intention or desire for God. A prayer word like "Jesus," "Father," or "Lord have mercy" can be used. We simply come to God by opening ourselves to him. We must not feel agitated or distracted when unwelcomed thoughts come knocking at our mind's door. We acknowledge their presence and let them go. If these thoughts keep coming in waves we can use the prayer word to redirect our attention to God.

We should not judge or expect something out of this period of solitude and silence. We may feel that we are wasting our time when nothing has happened. We will see the results later. We need

Desert of Transformation

to be patient and persevere in this discipline before we can reap the benefits. Gradually we find ourselves more at ease, more confident, and less fearful and anxious. Something has changed inside us without our knowledge. Thomas Keating, in his bestselling book *Open Mind, Open Heart*, has this to say:

> In this prayer God is speaking not to your ears, to your emotions, or to your head, but to your spirit, to your inmost being. There is no human apparatus to understand the language or to hear it. A kind of anointing takes place. The fruits of that anointing will appear later in ways that are indirect: in your calmness, in your peace, in your willingness to surrender to God in everything that happens.[18]

THE DESERTS OF OUR LIFE[19]

Most of us do not enter a literal desert to get rid of the false self. We can carve out an inner "desert" for ourselves instead. The discipline of solitude and silence will help to create a wilderness in our soul. The interior desert in us mirrors the external desert with its harsh conditions and empty spaces. We can enter the desert voluntarily or involuntarily. Metaphorically, a desert is any place where we face abandonment and isolation. Like Julian of Norwich, we can enter a desert involuntarily when faced with an illness, loss, or crisis in our life. When my wife received the bad news that she had ovarian cancer we were speechless and numbed by shock. We did not know how to respond to the bad news. The world that we had carefully constructed over the years came crashing down on us like a pile of bricks. We found ourselves transported to a place of desolation. We felt abandoned and left alone in a vast, empty space. We had indeed entered a desert involuntarily.

---

18. Keating, *Open Mind, Open Heart*, 83.

19. Material in this section is taken from my book *Being Truly Human*, 36–38.

Garden of the Soul

There is yet another way for us to enter a desert in our life. The desert can be anywhere where the familiar structures of the world have fallen apart—a desolated place filled with despair and little hope. It is an empty wasteland, forsaken and ignored by the world, where few people want to go. An AIDS hospital, a hospice for terminally ill patients, a mental asylum, a center for intellectually disabled children, a nursing home for the elderly and infirm, a counseling center for abused women and children, or a rehab center for drug addicts can become a desert for us. We learn to embrace the pain and suffering of the residents and share the solidarity of abandonment and nothingness with them in these desolated places. If we do that, we have carved out a "desert" for ourselves without entering a physical desert.

We all face different kinds of "deserts" in our life. To James Houston, professor of spirituality at Regent College, there is more than one kind of desert experience. Each personality with their own personal stories will face a different kind of desert experience. For example, the perfectionist will face a desert of imperfection. God will expose his weakness and give him the humility to walk through his failures. The giver will face the desert of inadequacy. In times of trouble, he is hard-pressed to seek help from others and God. The doer will face a desert of uselessness. He finds himself to be going nowhere and powerless to solve the problem he faces. The idealist will confront a desert of ordinariness. He finds life routine, boring, and lacking creativity. A desert of flux and disorientation is given to the rigid person that is afraid of change. The fun-lover will be transported to a desert place of pain and suffering to sober him down. The controller will face a desert of chaos and uncertainty. To the pleaser the desert will challenge him to confront reality and stand up for the truth.[20]

Any area of our life can be a potential desert. God will lead us through some deserts of our life if we are committed to grow spiritually and are willing to pay the price. Our life will be broken, shaped, and molded to conform to the image of Christ like a lump of clay before the sculptor. The emotional, bodily, economic,

---

20. Houston, *The Heart's Desire*, 178.

Desert of Transformation

vocational, and social aspects of our life will be at God's disposal to shape and mould us. We have our share of emotional deserts due to disappointments and expectations not met. Unfulfilled longings, memories of past hurts and abuses, and failed relationships can lead us to feel isolated and abandoned. It is difficult for us to share with others our pain and despair. Bodily deserts are caused by illness, accidents, and aging. The sudden loss of mobility will lead to a decline in the quality of life. We feel helpless and lonely when cut off from people and activities. Vocational deserts happen when we lose a job or when we have to stay in a job that we dislike deeply. We feel caged in by circumstances over which we have no control. We find ourselves adrift with no sense of direction or certainty in terms of our vocational goals. We also face economic deserts. The mountain of bills gets bigger; it is difficult to make ends meet. Faced with a financial crisis, we do not know where or whom to turn to. We become anxious in view of the accumulating financial debt. There are social deserts as well. Some of us keep changing friends and have not learned to hold on to a friendship for long. The friends that we have come to trust may have turned their backs against us when we need their help at a critical juncture of our life. Sometimes we can feel isolated and lonely even when there are people around us.[21]

THE TRANSFORMED LIFE

A lost person needs to value two important things in order to survive in the harsh environment of the desert. First, he must not panic. He must learn to ignore or be indifferent to the pain and despair that plague his mind. Then he needs to pay close attention to his surroundings to look for anything that can help to prolong his life. These two desert virtues of indifference and attentiveness are fundamental to the desert way of spirituality. Beldan Lane writes, "These two virtues are honed by exposure to the desert elements.

---

21. See Rensberger, "Deserted Spaces," 8–10.

The threat of the desert landscape has a way of eliciting the sharp, lean qualities of attentiveness and indifference."[22]

The desert, by virtue of its sparse emptiness, offers little to distract us. Our skills at observation are sharpened when honed by the desert environment. The senses are enhanced because our survival depends on them. Things that normally escape us in normal circumstances will attract our attention in the desert. The stars seem brighter and larger at night; the silence has substance and depth; the shadows more alive and threatening. We tend to notice things better when we move at a slow pace. There is no hurry in the desert. When the pace of life slows down we begin to see things around us for the very first time.

The twin gifts of indifference and attentiveness will pave the way for us to love freely. We are free when we are indifferent to the compulsions of life that the false self craves.[23] The true, authentic self is then free to love God and neighbor. To Jean Vanier, the road to freedom involves the gifts of indifference and attentiveness:

> We set out on the road to freedom when we no longer let our compulsions or passions govern us. We are freed when we begin to put justice, heartfelt relationships, and service of others and of truth over and above our own needs for love and success or our fears for failure and of relationships.[24]

We need humility and hospitality in order to love our neighbor. Humility is a way of life to the desert Christian. If pride of heart is the most serious sin, then humility is the most treasured virtue of the desert saints. It is a way of life for the desert Christian. In the famous Rule of St. Benedict that dictates the way of living for the monks, the chapter on humility is placed right in the middle. As Joan Chittister, herself a Benedictine nun, points out, that the chapter "leavens the entire document, the entire way life."[25] The

---

22. Lane, *Solace of Fierce Landscapes*, 188.
23. Mah, *Being Truly Human*, 55–56.
24. Vanier, *Becoming Human*, 115.
25. Chittister, *Wisdom Distilled from the Daily*, 52.

Desert of Transformation

humility of the desert is manifested in a willingness to learn from others and an unwillingness to stand in judgment of others.[26]

Abba Arsenius was a man of learning who received the best classical education available. He was once a personal tutor to the emperor's children. One day the monks were shocked to see him seeking advice from an Egyptian peasant about his thoughts. "How is it that you, with such good Latin and Greek education, ask this poor peasant about your thoughts?" they asked him. He replied saying, "I have indeed been taught Latin and Greek, but I do not know even the alphabet of this peasant."[27]

Abba Moses was called by the elders to an assembly in order to punish a brother who was guilty of a certain sin. He refused to enter the assembly. A priest went to him urging him to come, for the whole assembly was waiting for his presence. Then he arose taking with him an old, leaky basket filled with sand. He entered the assembly with the basket behind him. The assembly of brothers went out to meet him and saw the basket. "What is this, Father?" they asked. The old monk replied, "My sins are running behind me and I do not see them, and I have come today to judge the sins of another man." When they heard these words, they were touched and forgave the sinning brother.[28]

Hospitality is a virtue that belongs prominently to the desert. The need for mutual dependence in a wild, isolated place filled with unseen dangers and hardship fosters hospitality. It is a matter of mutual survival. No stranger is turned away in such an unforgiving environment with the mutual understanding that the same treatment will be given in return when needed in the future.[29] Abraham inviting the three angels of God to his tent for a meal is a fine example of desert hospitality (Gen 18:2–5).

Hospitality is more than sharing a meal or providing a bed for a guest. It is more an attitude, a habit of heart, than action. "It is," as Christine Pohl says in her book *Making Room*, "a welcome

---

26. Williams, "Gentle and Humble of Heart," 10–13.
27. Ward, *The Sayings of the Desert Fathers*, 10.
28. Waddell, trans., *The Desert Fathers*, 101–2.
29. Mah, *Being Truly Human*, 66.

with dispositions characterized by love and generosity."[30] It is more about making a room in our heart than finding a room in our house. It is to make ourselves available by giving the other person our undivided attention without imposing on her. To be fully present to the other person is not easy, for we often receive people with a divided mind. Sue Monk Kidd points this out:

> To be fully present is not to pass judgment on the other person, wanting to convert her to our point of view, desiring her appreciation, wondering what others may think, worrying about the weather, or generally getting caught up in one's own feeling, desires, and opinions of the moment.[31]

On his way to Jairius' house to attend to his dying daughter, Jesus' robe was touched by a woman seeking a cure from him. Jesus stopped in his tracks and created a hospitable space for the poor woman to tell her story. He looked at the woman and his eyes told her that he was there to listen to her story and share her pain without judgment and criticism. In the hospitable space given by Jesus, she found the freedom and courage to tell the painful truth and to confront her suffering that was in her heart for a long time. She heard these consoling words from Jesus: "Daughter, your faith has healed you. Go in peace and be freed from your suffering" (Mark 5:34). A change had taken place and she had shalom. She was healed not only physically but emotionally and spiritually as well.

Our availability to others in hospitality is the result of our availability to God first. Learning to wait upon God is a sign of our love for him. The desert has taught us the art of waiting. The desert saints, like Abraham, had learned the hard lesson of waiting upon God. God promised Abraham a child at age seventy. After eleven years he took matters into his own hands and had Ishmael through his slave Hagar. He was forced to wait for another fourteen years before Isaac was born. David had to wait for more than ten years

---

30. Pohl, *Making Room*, 152.
31. Kidd, "Live Welcoming to All," 9.

before he could be king of Israel after his victory over Goliath. Moses had to wait for forty years shepherding sheep in the desert before God chose him to lead Israel out of Egypt. We too have to learn to abandon our self to God's love and wait to receive from God whatever he wants to give to us or take from us. Waiting also involves our willingness to walk in his ways and not our ways. The psalmist exhorts us to "wait for the Lord and keep his way" (Ps 37:34). When we wait and walk before God we will find ourselves gradually transformed to Christ-likeness. Jesus too learned to wait and walk in his mission for God on earth. Often he told his disciples that his time had not yet come and he also told them that he had come to do the will of his Father. Waiting and walking are two precious lessons that we learn from the desert.[32]

Conclusion

The desert is an ideal place for the nurturing of the soul. The ruggedness of the place calls for a rugged faith in its inhabitants. The soul can divert its attention to God when detached from the world and its pleasures. In the desert, our greatest enemy is the darkness that resides in our heart. We need to do battle in the wilderness of our soul to dethrone the false self in order to give space for God to do the work of transformation in our heart. We can carve out a "desert" in our life through the discipline of solitude and silence. A desert can be anywhere where the familiar structures of the world have fallen apart—a desolate place filled with despair and little hope. We can voluntarily enter into one of these deserts that are around us. The desert will teach us the twin virtues of attentiveness and indifference. The result is a freedom to love God and to love our neighbor. Love requires us to show humility and hospitality to our neighbor. This is only possible if we love God first through waiting on him in order to will and walk in all his ways.

---

32. Mulholland, "Life in the Desert," 26–27.

QUESTIONS TO CONSIDER AND REFLECT

1. In what ways is the desert a preferred place to train God's servants?

2. Why is it difficult to spend a short time in solitude and silence? Why is solitude and silence essential to your spiritual life? Can you think of some ways you can have solitude and silence in your busy life?

3. Can you identify some of the "deserts" in your life? Was there a time in your life when God seemed distant and your confidence, hope, faith, and trust were taken from you and you became "nothing"? What was it like to experience abandonment in your life?

4. Hospitality is to make ourselves available and be fully present to the other person. How has this definition of hospitality change the way you deal with people?

6

Mountain of Challenge

One climbs a mountain drawn instinctively by the magnetism of the highest point, as to a summit of personal awareness, awareness of oneself as a point in relation to as much of space as can be grasped within a maximal horizon. Thus a mountain top is one of the most sensitive spots on earth.

—TIM ROBINSON[1]

THE APPEAL OF MOUNTAINS

THOSE WHO HAVE CLIMBED a mountain speak of a transcendent experience. A demanding landscape requires full concentration and total involvement for its participants, resulting in a deep bond and camaraderie among the climbers. It is a holistic feeling that comes about when one is deeply and intimately involved with its environment. Many climbers use the word "flow" to describe

---

1. Robinson, *Setting Foot on the Shores of Connemara*, 163–64.

their experience.[2] Flow happens when one action flows to another without the need for conscious intervention to evaluate and assess. One is suspended in timelessness when there is no distinction between past, present, and future. There is also no distinction between the self and the environment and between stimulus and response. The perception in terms of the self, others, and the environment changes as a result of the climb. The unencumbered self during this time is free from self-awareness and other limitations, leading to the emergence of the true self. This loss of ego leads to a diminished sense of self.

The mountain carries an attraction and a sense of appeal to many people. A typical response when we ask a climber why he climbs the mountain is that the mountain is there. Scaling the peak may be the obvious reason to climb a mountain but deep down our need for transcendence draws us to climb a mountain. Some of the famous Taoist and Buddhist temples in China are located on high mountains. China has five great mountains, which are all religious sites. The emperors of China, in the past, had to make pilgrimages to these sites, especially Mount Tai, which was and still is the most important of the five mountains. Mount Tai, a UNESCO World Heritage Site, is located in Shandong Province and is above five thousand feet high. It was the official site for the emperor to pay an annual homage—to heaven at the summit and to earth at the foot of the mountain.

The early monasteries in Europe were built on mountainous sites that were not easily accessible to the public. Saint Bruno, with a handful of French monks, went to the mountainous Alps to build an isolated monastery. That was the first community of the Carthusian order. A visitor once commented that the path to the isolated monastery was a frightening experience because on one side of the path was a steep precipice and on the other side was the hanging rock above. Apparently the path was carved out of the steep, rocky slope of the mountain. Basil of Caesarea, one of the Cappadocian Fathers of the Eastern church, once visited the desert monks in Syria and Egypt in the fourth century. Upon his return, he decided

---

2. Mitchell, *Mountain Experience*, 153–69.

to duplicate the harsh landscapes of the desert by building his small monastery in mountainous Cappadocia. Eventually Cappadocia was known for its many churches and monasteries that were built high up in the mountains.[3] The early Christians used these mountainous hideouts to escape persecutions before Christianity became a legal religion. A vast network of underground cities was built to fend off any intruders through the use of creative traps and narrow tunnels.

This deep desire for transcendence also led men to build another kind of mountain in the twelve century. It was a man-made massive structure that rose above the landscape and dwarfed all the buildings around it at the time it was built. The smart use of geometric dimensions and light make the Gothic cathedral a unique place of worship. The mathematic principles of symmetry and harmonious proportions are painstakingly applied to the design and structure of the building. Its cross-ribbed vault grows like branches of trees sprouting skyward and forms the roof of the cathedral. This gives the onlooker a sense of awe and wonder. The walls are no longer used to support the massive roof as in the older buildings. Pillars now support the roof instead. Large openings are punched along the thin walls to allow light to enter the building. Stained glass windows provide the luminous sense that God's grace is pouring into the sanctuary. The Gothic cathedral strives to make an earthly form of the heavenly image. It is a kind of celestial city on earth. Man does not need to go up to a mountain to get a vision of God. He now needs to enter the Gothic cathedral to be transported to heaven.[4]

The mountains mentioned in the Bible are usually sites of transcendent spiritual experiences. Abraham's faith was severely tested when God told him to sacrifice his only son, Isaac. Abraham went to the place God had told him about and he tied up his son and laid him on the wood. God stopped him from doing the unthinkable by providing a ram caught in the thicket by its horns. Later the place was called "On the mountain of the Lord

---

3. Lane, *The Solace of Fierce Landscapes*, 48, 47.
4. Mah, *Being Truly Human*, 29.

it will be provided" (Gen 22:9–14). God spoke to Moses from a burning bush. He was led to this place while tending the sheep of his father-in-law. He led the flock to the far side of the desert to Horeb, the mountain of God. There he saw a bush on fire but it did not burn up (Exod 3:1–2). Later Moses was taken to Mount Sinai and went in a cloud to meet God face to face (Exod 19). Elijah too had his mountain-top experience when he encountered God on the same site that Moses heard God speak from the bush. Earlier at Mount Carmel, he fought hard against the Baal worshippers and saw fire from heaven come down to consume the sacrifices (1 Kgs 18:36–39). At Horeb he heard God asking him what he was doing there. Then he was instructed by God to go back from where he came and given tasks to do (1 Kgs 19:9–18). Jesus used to go to a solitary place in the mountain to pray (John 6:15). He was transfigured at Mount Tabor before the eyes of his three disciples. His face shone like the sun and his clothes became as white as light. Moses and Elijah appeared and talked with Jesus. God spoke from a bright cloud indicating his pleasure for the Son and called on the disciples to listen to him (Matt 7:1–5).

Mountains that rise skyward are luminal places between the earthly and the heavenly. Early saints like John of the Cross and John Climacus used the image of ascending a mountain to depict the spiritual life. John of the Cross wrote *Ascent of Mount Carmel* in which he describes the different types of landscapes that God uses to stir the will. The better it is for the soul's development if the landscape is more austere, solitary, and wild. John Climacus wrote *The Ladder of Divine Ascent* which explains in detail the way of purgation and the problem of vice that prevents the development of the believer's spiritual life. He wrote this book at the request of a fellow abbot who said, "Tell us in our ignorance what, like Moses of old, you have seen in divine vision upon the mountain; write it down in a book and send it to us as if it were the tablets of the Law, written by God."[5]

---

5. John, *The Ladder of Divine Ascent*, 12.

AT THE FOOTHILLS

Not many people will want to climb the mountain. Many prefer life at the foothills. Life is safer, less risky, and more predictable at the foot of the mountain. Even the psalmist senses the danger when he climbs the hills. He reminds himself that God is there to help him in case he slips. He will watch his every step night and day. He begins the psalm with a call for help: "I lift up my eyes to the hills—where does my help come from? My help comes from the Lord, the Maker of heaven and earth." He ends the psalm with this assurance: "The Lord will keep you from all harm—he will watch over your life; the Lord will watch over your coming and going both now and forevermore" (Ps 121:1–2; 7–8). This psalm was frequently on my lips when I travelled by bus on the mountain roads in Nepal. The mountain roads in Nepal are prone to accidents and tragic fatalities. Most of the mountain roads are narrow, lacking guardrails, and not paved with tar or even gravel. The buses are usually overloaded with people and goods. It is not unusual to see passengers, especially young men, taking to the roof of the bus in order to get some fresh air or a better view. It takes a strong heart to travel on those treacherous roads in Nepal.

Why are Christians not making the ascent? Some people think that the Christian life is like a stroll in a park.[6] They are given the impression that a Christian's life is a life of peace, happiness, and prosperity. They will soon find out that the spiritual life is more than a stroll; it is like a marathon that requires effort, training, and sacrifice to run the race. They do not expect this and are not prepared to run the entire race. Many prefer life at the foothills in the face of unpreparedness and false expectations. They are not ready for the rigors and challenges that the spiritual journey requires. Other Christians think that their conversion is the goal of their spiritual life, assuming that they have finished running the race once they experience conversion. In fact the race has barely begun. There is a lot of work to be done in order for them to fulfill the call of God to be holy as he is holy.

---

6. McGrath, *The Journey*, 9.

Leo Tolstoy, a Russian novelist and religious writer, is a good example. Tolstoy had a conversion experience and he assumed that with this experience he had completed the journey of faith. He underestimated the power of sin in his life that could hinder his spiritual growth and did not take seriously the need to deal with his flawed personality and be transformed inwardly. Oblivious to his weakness, he made himself a spokesman on what was proper Christian conduct and wrote articles attacking the Russian Orthodox Church for her shortcomings. He thought he could "move from conversion to the love of neighbor in one giant step" because of his wonderful conversion experience. Diogenes Allen, in his book *Spiritual Theology*, remarks that the gap between conversion and loving the neighbor "are separated by a vast distance that can only gradually be closed with considerable effort and help."[7]

It is interesting to note that the two Greek words for "mountain" and "limit, boundary" are the same except for the breath mark. *Horos*, with the hard breath mark, means "mountain," whereas *oros*, with the soft breath mark, (without *h*) means "limit, boundary."[8] A mountain is a natural boundary because it prevents people from one side going over to the other side. Hence, mountains make good geographical markers and the size and shape of many nations are formed by mountainous terrain. The mountain itself presents a limit to those who want to climb it. Not many have the stamina or the courage to climb a high mountain. Many give up before reaching the top. This limit is self-imposed. There is another limit that is imposed by others. Certain mountains, for whatever reasons, are not accessible to the public. At Mount Sinai the Lord put a limit to his holy mountain. Only Moses and Aaron were allowed to scale the mountain. The priests had to consecrate themselves if they wanted to approach the Lord on the mountain. The people were warned to stay away and remain at the foot of God's mountain (Exod 19:20–5).

What separates the people who live at the foothills and those who scale mountains? Walker Percy, a metaphysician and novelist,

---

7. Allen, *Spiritual Theology*, 8.
8. Thurston, *The Spiritual Landscape of Mark*, 41.

once said, "I have learned that the most important difference between people is those for whom life is a quest and those for whom it is not."[9] Those who make the journey have a richer experience and exposure than those who prefer to stay behind. They will discover the mysterious work of God in their lives beyond familiar boundaries. They will live at a higher level of risk and challenge. A sedentary life at the foothills is safe, predictable, and less risky, but it lacks the challenge that the summit brings to those who through much preparation, hardship, and sacrifice are able to reach the top. From this vantage point we see life differently. Probably this was the reason why Jesus took three of his disciples to go up Mount Tabor. I am sure that Peter, James, and John, having been at the summit and experienced a vision of God, would come down from the mountain with a greater sense of purpose and resolve in their mission to follow Jesus. "We climb mountains," writes Margaret Silf, "to gain a different perspective on our lives and our world. In short, climbing mountains leads us to a new vision."[10]

JOURNEY OF FAITH

This new vision can only be achieved when we embark on a journey of faith. A journey requires preparation. It is not a preparation in terms of what to bring and what not to bring along. It is more a preparation of the heart to trust God for any eventualities. Jesus instructed his disciples to take nothing for the journey when he sent them to the villages to heal and to proclaim the kingdom of God. They were told not to take along staff, bag, bread, money, not even a tunic. They needed to trust God for the hospitality of the people they met along the way (Mark 6:7–13). It is a journey of faith because it presupposes both a destination and the place they leave behind. It is leaving familiar territory and moving into unfamiliar boundaries.

---

9. Quoted in Allen, *Spiritual Theology*, 23.
10. Silf, *Landscapes of Prayer*, 17.

Garden of the Soul

The mountain scenery and climate change as the altitude increases. Kilimanjaro, Africa's highest mountain, which is located at the equator, has five climate zones. The tropical lower slopes, below 6,000 feet, are cultivated with coffee and banana. The next zone, from 6,000 to 9,000 feet, is the rainforest, which receives the highest amount of rain. Next is the moorland, which is covered with heather and bright flowers. Above the moorland is the high desert with its harsh conditions and extreme temperatures ranging from mid eighties to below freezing at night. The summit zone, beginning at 16,500 feet above sea level, is an icy wasteland where glaciers can be found. Here the air is thin, with half as much oxygen as at sea level. It is easy for a mountaineer to experience acute mountain sickness at such high altitudes. It is necessary for the body to adjust to the changing conditions presented by the mountain as the climber makes his ascent. Jon Krakauer, a mountaineer, writes:

> The human body adjusts in manifold ways, from increasing respiration, to changing pH of the blood, to radically boosting the number of oxygen-carrying red blood cells—a conversion that takes weeks to complete.[11]

The changes experienced by the human body have their spiritual counterparts in the soul's ascent to God. Like the human body, our faith through the journey to the top will be challenged and strengthened. Our capacity for God needs to be stretched in order for us to catch the vision at the summit. This means that before we are ready to summit we must undergo the rigors of the climb. Most experienced mountaineers do not summit in the shortest time possible. They will make a few descents to lower elevations to acclimatize their bodies before they make the final push to the top. The journey is as important as the destination to the experienced climber. We can be so focused on the goal of our journey that we have lost its significance in terms of our personal growth and development in the faith. The rigors of the ascent will strengthen our

---

11. Krakauer, *Into Thin Air*, 90.

faith and enlarge our vision of God. The journey itself is already a destination though the goal of the journey is to make the summit.

Peterson relates the story of traveling with a friend on a spectacular mountain road. While on the road, his friend was not interested in the scenic wonders around her: a majestic waterfall, a glacier formation, a grove of massive cedars, mountains on a distant horizon. She kept looking at her map and hardly looked up. She wanted to know the direction they were going and make sure that they were on course to the destination. She had lost sight of the most important part of the journey because getting to the destination was her main concern.[12] We have no time to savor and enjoy the journey when we are in a hurry to get to our destination. One day I was walking with my students to a retreat hideout. Instead of taking the tram car to the top of Penang Hill, we decided to take a slow walk up the hill where the bungalow was. I did not expect the trip to take so long. I was getting slightly impatient. A member of our group took her sweet time to pause and take notice of the things along the way. She was taking her time to enjoy the sights and sounds of the forest trail. I was anxious about reaching the destination on time. She sensed my impatience and remarked, "It is not the destination but the journey that makes it worthwhile." I got the message. We often pay scant attention to the things that happen around us when in a hurry to go somewhere.[13] Robert Pirsig writes:

> To live only for some future goals is shallow. It is the sides of the mountain which sustains life, not the top. Here's where things grow. But of course, without the top you can't have the sides. It's the top that defines the sides.[14]

---

12. Peterson, *The Way of Jesus*, 40.

13. Mah, *Being Truly Human*, 55.

14. Pirsig, *Zen and the Art of Motorcycle Maintenance*, 198, quoted in Peterson, *The Way of Jesus*, 41.

Garden of the Soul

THE CLIMB TO THE TOP

In the Oxherding Pictures of Zen Buddhism, one stage of the journey shows the farmer trying to catch the ox in order to tame and ride on it. The farmer is being dragged to and fro by the ox when it resists his efforts to tame it. The ox is finally under his control after much patience and whipping. A harness is placed through its nose. The wild nature of the beast is tamed and it is now a gentle creature willing to be led by the master. He is now able to climb on its back and with great joy rides the ox home. The ox represents the farmer's own wild, untamed animal nature that needs to be under control. The farmer must learn to overcome his own wild, untamed nature in order to become the sort of person that the great ox will allow on its back.[15]

In Dante's *Divine Comedy*, the pilgrim who wakes up in the dark wood sees the mountain of purgatory before him. He rushes to the gate hoping to begin his journey up the mountain that leads to paradise. At the gate he discovers that the entrance is blocked by fierce-looking animals. These ferocious animals represent the degraded, beastly creature he has become. He calls out to Virgil, who is sent to be his guide through much of the journey up the mountain. He cries out that he will be destroyed by his own animal nature. In order to take this path of grace up the mountain, the pilgrim needs to confront his own sinful nature and to deal aggressively with the besetting sins that hinder him from making this journey. The path up the purgatory mountain has seven terraces that represent the seven deadly sins. Each terrace provides a challenge for the pilgrim to overcome and to turn away from his sins. The proud will bend down to look at the floor due to the weights tied to his body. Those who are consumed by anger will walk through thick dark smoke and the lustful will pass through burning flames to get to Beatrice, the object of the pilgrim's infatuation. The first steps up the mountain can be the most challenging for the pilgrim. As the journey proceeds it becomes less terrifying as his faith gets stronger. The gravity of sin that pulls him down

---

15. Morris, "Riding the Wild Mountain Ox" 8, 10.

Mountain of Challenge

and makes the journey difficult becomes lighter as the journey progresses.[16]

The trick, as Virgil points out, is not to look back but to keep moving forward. Climbing a mountain requires perseverance. A stream never looks back; it keeps moving forward. When confronting a rock, a stream always wins not because of its strength but through perseverance. Two frogs are found inside a barrel of cream. They try hard to jump out of the barrel, but each time they slip back into the cream because the side is too slippery and steep. One of the frogs decides to give up trying. He slowly sinks into the cream and drowns. The other frog keeps trying. His continued kicking eventually turns the cream into solid butter. He is able to jump out of the barrel with one final leap. His perseverance pays for his freedom.[17]

John Climacus's *Ladder of Divine Assent* suggests a variety of spiritual exercises to help the pilgrim overcome and purge his deadly sins. These ascetic exercises require perseverance and are not for the faint-hearted. Vigorous self-denial is used to curb the fleshly appetites and to detach from worldly concerns over money, possessions, glory, and relationships. It is important that the pilgrim does all these with the help of God's grace and not based on his own human effort alone. To purge sins the pilgrim must dig deep into those unconscious attachments that are not easily noticed or detected in his life. God will sometimes use darkness and suffering to do his work of transformation for sins that are lodged deep inside the heart.[18] Thomas Merton, the mystic and Trappist monk, has this advice for us: "We need to leave the initiative in the hands of God working in our souls either directly in the night of aridity and suffering, or through events and other men."[19]

God's work is to transform us into the likeness of Christ. By overcoming we become more like Christ. We are "to become mature, attaining to the whole measure of the fullness of Christ"

16. Barnes, *Search for Home*, 73, 107–8.
17. Hughes, *7 Laws of Spiritual Success*, 66–68.
18. Sittser, *Water from a Deep Well*, 172–73.
19. Merton, *New Seeds of Contemplation*, 257.

(Eph 3:13). We are made to bear the image of Christ. To bear the image of Christ fully is to satisfy our deep inner hunger and thirst for wholeness. While living in this fractured world, we look for all sorts of substitutes to fill up the emptiness in our human spirit. We look for meaning and purpose in life by assuming a variety of roles and identities. We want more and look for more things to possess and do to fill this emptiness with the hope that much doing, wanting, and having will numb the pain and fill the void in our heart. We should know by now that all these will end in failure because the heart, like the grave, is never satisfied. Only the image of Christ can bring healing, restoration, and wholeness in our life. Our fractured life torn by indifference, resentment, defensiveness, manipulation, and unfaithfulness will be replaced by compassion, forgiveness, kindness, and openness.[20] The task of the spiritual life is to obey the two commandments: to love God and to love one's neighbor. Fulfilling this task will lead to the goal of our spiritual journey: to catch a vision of God.

SUMMIT OF VISION

We are familiar with the story of Jesus taking three of his disciples to scale Mount Tabor. Jesus was transfigured before their very eyes at the mountaintop. His clothes became dazzling white and his face shone like the sun. A bright cloud suddenly appeared and enveloped Moses and Elijah while they were talking to Jesus. A voice within the cloud was heard telling the disciples to listen to Jesus for he was God's Son whom the Father loved. The disciples, on seeing this sight and hearing the voice, fell to the ground terrified (Matt 17:1–6). This Bible story provides the inspiration for Theophanes the Greek to paint an icon of the transfiguration in the second half of the fourteenth century. It is a masterpiece of geometric forms and theological subtlety. The geometric forms that are used to depict the perfect and the eternal make the scene unearthly. The icon can be divided into two halves. The upper half

---

20. Mulholland, *Invitation to a Journey*, 34.

shows Jesus, Moses, and Elijah standing individually on pointed mountains. Jesus is pictured at the center, accompanied by Moses and Elijah in bowed supplication. The peaceful setting of the upper half is in marked contrast with the subdued mood of the lower half. The three apostles, greatly disturbed by the dynamic display of bright light and a sudden voice, are pictured bending towards the ground. The impact throws the apostles to the ground with Peter trying to use his hand to shield his face from the dazzling light. The other two disciples turn their faces away from the vision with James using his hand to cover his eyes. The disciples have seen the glory of God manifested right before their eyes.

When Moses asked God to show him his glory, God answered that no one might see his face and live. Moses had to hide in a cleft of a rock with the hand of God covering him when God's glory passed by him (Exod 33:18–23). It is foolish for us to look directly at the blazing sun with our naked eyes. Things are best viewed in diffused light. The white light refracted through a prism or glass provides brilliant colorful images that please instead of piercing the eyes. This is the reason why the light of God's revelation in Scripture is best conveyed and refracted through the colorful rays of metaphor, story, parable, imagery, analogy, poetry, and symbol.[21]

Luci Shaw explains that the full vision of God's glory will be too much for her without the protective shield of imagery or veil of metaphor. "God, knowing our frailty, parcels out truth to us in small gifts of metaphor, and reveals himself to us in clumps of words, in the sacraments, in the natural theology of Creation." A Presbyterian friend of hers was heard telling his colleague that all the liturgical apparatus in the Anglican Church was distracting him from a direct experience of God. His friend agreed and replied with the remark that God was too glorious to be apprehended directly. He further explained that the liturgy, the robes, the incense, and the chanting were to enable the worshipper to stand in God's presence without being bowled over by the power.[22]

21. Shaw, "The Need to Pay Attention," 18.
22. Ibid., 20.

Garden of the Soul

The way to get a glimpse of God's vision is not through our physical eyes but through the readiness of our heart. If our hearts are not opened we may have eyes and not see and have ears but not hear. Jesus says that only the pure in heart can see God. God becomes visible to us when our heart is pure. Peterson in his *Message* paraphrases the words of Jesus in Matthew 13:10–13 concerning the use of parables to convey truth:

> Whenever someone has a ready heart for this, the insights and understanding flow freely. But if there is no readiness, any trace of receptivity soon disappears. That's why I tell stories: to create readiness, to nudge the people toward receptive insight.[23]

According to Gregory of Nyssa, a Cappadocian theologian of the fourth century, we will never reach the goal of our journey. The spiritual life is a life of ceaseless growth and change. We will never stop growing in the likeness of Christ, for life on earth is imperfect. We only achieve perfection when we leave this world and going to the next. This does not mean that we should stop trying to scale the summit and catch a glimpse of God's vision. Even the disciples after the dramatic vision on top of Mount Tabor had to come down to the world below to continue with their work of the kingdom. In our lifetime there will be many mountains to climb and summits to conquer. Each mountain challenges our faith and greatly increases our capacities for God in our hearts. As we overcome the besetting sins in our life and become more and more like Christ—overflowing with love for God and neighbor—our receptive insight for God increases.

This "vision" leads us to know God. The more we know God the more we become like him and grow in love for God is love. This union of relationship is just like the love relationship between the beloved and lover in the Song of Songs. Bernard of Clairvaux extolled the love relationship between Christ and his church in his many sermons on the Song of Songs. According to him, God's love for us implants in us a desire to love God in return. Our love for

---

23. Peterson, *The Message*, 41.

God does not blossom overnight. It grows by degree. There are four degrees of love. As creatures of the flesh, we love ourselves for our own sake. This is the first degree. The next level is to love God for our own sake. We realize that we need God and he is able to meet our needs. Then we graduate to the third degree of love when we love God for God's sake. We begin to think of God's goodness and love him for who he is and not what he can give to us. Lastly, we love ourselves for God's sake. In the state of the simplicity and purity of intention the heart's desire is not its own but God's. He cares for himself because he loves God and only that God wants him to have it. Abba Isaac has these words for us concerning the union of the believer with the Father and Son:

> And this will come to pass when God shall be all our love, and every desire and wish and effort, every thought of ours, and all our life and words and breath, and that unity which already exists between the Father and the Son, and the Son and the Father, has been shed abroad in our hearts and minds, so that as He loves us with a pure and unfeigned and indissoluble love, so we also may be joined with Him by a lasting and inseparable affection.[24]

Peter found a project to do after the transfiguration at Mount Tabor. He proposed that they built three shelters for Jesus, Moses, and Elijah. He wanted to remain behind and was not willing to go back to the world below. This was not possible because the journey needed to continue on. He needed to come down from the mountain to a world waiting for him to labor and love. This extraordinary encounter at the mountaintop prepared him for the ordinary matters of life in the world below. A large crowd mobbed around Jesus and the disciples, bringing with them their usual complaints and problems, when they came down from the mountain. Jesus had to deal with the crowd like before. The world had not changed a lot since the time they went up the mountain. What had changed was that the disciples were now able to plunge deeper into the world as Christ's servants bearing the love of God in their hearts.

---

24. Cassian, *Conferences*, 11: 404.

Having seen Jesus at the transfiguration, they were now able to see the beloved Jesus not only in themselves but in others as well.[25]

Jesus says that only the pure in heart can see and know God. A heart free of the illusions of self allows itself to dwell with God in the full embrace of his love. Such a life will impact others. Others will experience themselves as the beloved of God in the presence of such people. Having met Mother Theresa, Basil Pennington can testify to this:

> This morning I sat across the table and looked into the eyes of Mother Theresa in Calcutta that is forever etched in my soul. That morning I came to know, love, and respect myself as a Christ-person, the beloved of God.[26]

Conclusion

The ascent up the mountain is a metaphor for our spiritual journey. The mountain has always been a challenge and inspiration to many as long as there are people who are on a spiritual quest. Though the mountain has a special appeal, many people will rather stay at the foothills than face the daunting task of scaling the mountain to reach its top. If we want to grow in our spiritual life we need to embark on a journey of faith even though climbing is risky and requires much preparation and sacrifice. Though reaching the summit is the journey's goal, the journey is its destination. As we journey we learn to overcome the sins that are plaguing us and slowly become more like Christ. Like the human body that needs to adapt to the changes in altitude and terrain, the soul too will align itself more and more to the presence and will of God. Our capacity for God expands with the increase of faith. We begin to gain a different perspective of our lives and our world. Our vision of God leads us to know and love God more intimately. Embraced by the love of God, we too are able to serve his kingdom through

---

25. Pennington, "Tabor: Icon of Contemplation," 35.
26. Pennington, "Bernard's Challenge," 23.

loving our neighbor. We will find our lives making an impact on others in ways that we do not plan or expect.

QUESTIONS TO CONSIDER AND REFLECT

1. Where does this desire for transcendence come from? What would you do to satisfy this need?
2. Do you see life as a quest? Would you rather scale a mountain than live at the foothills? What might prevent you from taking up this journey of faith?
3. When you travel, are you more concerned about reaching your destination or taking time to enjoy the journey itself? Is it important to know the difference?
4. What does it take to catch a vision of God? What difference does it make to your life when you have this vision?

Conclusion

IN THIS BOOK, THE journey of our soul begins in the garden and ends on the summit of the mountain. Along the way we are faced with many challenges and opportunities. We are warned of the pitfalls that can undermine our spiritual growth, and we are also given tips on how to grow our soul successfully. As the saying goes, the journey of a thousand miles begins with the first step. Many Christians, unfortunately, prefer life at the foothills or staying close to the shore, rather than cross a sea, climbing a mountain, or transiting a desert. They have not taken the first step to begin the journey of faith. Paul compares physical training with the training in godliness and says that though attention given to the physical body has some value, godly training has an even greater value because it affects everything we do now and has eternal consequences (1 Tim 4:8). If so much time and money are given to keep our body fit, why do Christians not pay equal time and energy to their soul? There are several reasons for this.

First, we do not want to take unnecessary risks. Embarking on a journey of faith requires us to leave our familiar territory and go beyond unknown boundaries. The future cannot be predicted and is totally unknown to us. This is why the journey has to be undertaken by faith. Even if the modern person is ready to take calculated risks, he makes sure that he is adequately covered by insurance. He wants coverage from any damages caused by nature (famines, floods, earthquakes, plagues) or caused by humans interfering with nature (bird flu, nuclear fallout, wars, terrorism). As

Conclusion

Anthony Giddens, in his book *Runaway World*, points out, people are willing to take risks if they are adequately insured but "insurance is conceivable only where we believe in a humanly engineered future."[1] The spiritual life requires us to yield to God's ways and meet him on his terms. We have no say in the future shape and direction of the journey we are taking. Like Abraham who was called to enter Canaan, he had no idea what was in store for him on the other side. We are not willing to take uncalculated risk and hand over the control of our future to someone else. This is why we are hesitant to take up the challenge to begin the journey.

Second, we are used to shortcuts while living in a technological society. We are always looking for ways to do things efficiently with the least time and minimal resources. This is possible and much welcomed in a material world. One way to judge whether a country is making any progress in the modern sense is to see the size of the working force in the agriculture sector. If the size of the working population shrinks in the agriculture sector and more workers are in the service sector this is a good sign that the nation is heading in the right direction. With the introduction of highly efficient technology, the size of the knowledge workers will increase with a correspondent decrease in the size of the labor-intensive workers. We cannot adopt this mentality in terms of our spiritual life. There are no shortcuts or techniques we can adopt to grow our soul. Spiritual growth, like physical growth, is a process and takes time. The process can be tedious and difficult at times and there is no magic formula to hasten the process of growth. We do face setbacks and failures along the way, but we need to persevere to the end. This journey of the soul is too daunting for some who lack the patience to work through the process of growth.

Third, we live a hurried life. Our life is packed with activities. Time is no longer a gift from God that we can enjoy but a commodity that we can use and maximize. In order to make full use of our time, we run from one activity to another. This running about should give us a good feeling since we thrive on doing rather than being. We feel guilty, bored, and useless if we have ample time on

1. Giddens, *Runaway World*, 25.

our hands. Too many activities can crowd out the space for God in our hearts. The Bible says that we are to be still in order to know God. Peterson feels that hurry is a "form of violence practiced on time."[2] Hurry also does violence to our soul's growth. We should pause in the midst of our busyness to reset and resonate ourselves to the rhythms that God has set in our life and in the world around us. Any kind of spiritual growth needs space and time and all forms of hurry are the soul's worst enemies. Sabbath keeping is good for our soul because it protects us from being swamped by the tyranny of hurried time. For many, the lack of time due to a hurried life is the main cause why they are not ready to pay much attention to the growth of their soul.

Fourth, we live a shallow, superficial life that lacks direction and purpose. Not rooted or grounded to a permanent center, we feel adrift and restless. Change is a permanent feature of our modern lifestyle and we tend to live only for the future. This tendency causes anxieties and angst in our life and we find it tough to focus and concentrate on the essential and necessary. We are easily distracted and succumb to temporal satisfactions. In a mobile and rootless society, it is difficult to forge lasting relationships knowing that we will not be in the same place for long. A person moves from place to place, job to job, relationship to relationship, picking up different identities and roles along the way. This plurality of roles and identities make modern living stressful and empty of meaning and purpose. In this context, it is difficult to make any long-term commitment to a cause or relationship. Spiritual growth demands a measure of commitment and sacrificial discipline from the participant. Many people, due to the lack of commitment and discipline, are put off by the serious demands of the spiritual life.

Fifth, we live an addictive life. Scott Peck, in his book *The Road Less Travelled*, acknowledges that one of the great truths of life is that life is difficult.[3] Unless a person comes to terms with this he will not be able to solve life's problems with the tools of discipline. Life can be tough, and one way to avoid the anxieties and

2. Peterson, *Answering God*, 61.
3. Peck, *The Road Less Travelled*, 13.

Conclusion

stresses of modern life is to seek refuge in one's addictions. Such addictions can shield and numb us from the painful realities of life. They allow us to hang on to the illusions of life while we refuse to face the pain that life mercilessly offers us from time to time. We prefer to escape into a world of dreams, fantasies, and illusions. The authentic spiritual life is grounded in reality. The growth of our spiritual life requires us to adhere to a set of disciplines or a rule of life that sets us on course to deal with the painful realities of sin in our life. Sin, according to the Bible, is the source of life's problems and difficulties. We cannot grow the spiritual life if we live an addictive life.

To undertake this journey, from the garden to the summit on a mountain, is not easy. We must be willing to take the necessary risk to allow God to order the shape and direction of the journey. The journey can be difficult and requires commitment and discipline on our part to make it a success. Meanwhile, we need to trust in the grace of God and not on our own efforts to help us grow the spiritual life. We must be prepared for the long and tedious journey ahead of us for there are no shortcuts to the nurturing of our soul. Much time and effort are used to grow the soul and patience and perseverance are needed. Knowing that all kinds of addictions will hinder our spiritual walk with God, we need to identify them and get rid of them in our life. We must be ready to confront the harsh realities of life and use the tools of discipline to deal with life's problems and difficulties. A rule of life, prayerfully implemented, will go a long way to provide discipline and structure to our spiritual growth.

George Bernard Shaw, Irish playwright and writer, once said that "the best way to seek God is in the garden. You can dig for him there." The garden of our soul needs tending. With prolonged toil and tears, the garden will grow to our joy and delight. The fragrant flowers and fruitful plants in the garden of our soul are the virtues that bring much delight and pleasure to God. This will invoke God to come often to the garden of our soul so that we can fellowship and seek him there. We are made for this purpose: to glorify God and enjoy him forever.

Bibliography

Abbey, Edward. *Desert Solitaire: A Season in the Wilderness.* New York: Ballantine, 1968.
Allen, Diogenes. *Spiritual Theology: The Theology of Yesterday for Spiritual Help Today.* Cambridge: Cowley, 1997.
Aristotle. *The Rhetoric and the Poetics of Aristotle.* Introduction by Edward P. J. Corbett. New York: Modern Library, 1984.
Augustine. *City of God.* In vol. 2 of *Nicene and Post Nicene-Fathers*, ser. 1, edited by Philip Schaff. Peabody, MA: Hendrickson, 1995.
———. *On the Morals of the Catholic Church.* In vol. 4 of *Nicene and Post Nicene-Fathers*, ser. 1, edited by Philip Schaff. Peabody, MA: Hendrickson, 1995.
Bakke, Jeannette A. *Holy Invitations: Exploring Spiritual Direction.* Grand Rapids: Baker, 2000.
Barnes, M. Craig. *Searching for Home: Spirituality for Restless Souls.* Grand Rapids: Brazos, 2003.
Basil of Caesarea, *Hexaemeron.* In vol. 8 of *Nicene and Post-Nicene Fathers*, ser. 2, edited by Philip Schaff and Henry Wace. Peabody, MA: Hendrickson, 1995.
Baxter, Richard. *The Saints' Everlasting Rest.* London: Epworth, 1962.
Bell, Luke. *A Deep and Subtle Joy: Life at Quarr Abbey.* Leominster: Gracewing, 2006.
Benner, David G. *Opening to God: Lectio Divina and Life as Prayer.* Downers Grove, IL: InterVarsity, 2010.
———. *Soulful Spirituality: Becoming Fully Alive and Deeply Human.* Grand Rapids: Brazos, 2011.
Bloom, Anthony. *Beginning to Pray.* New York: Paulist, 1970.
Bonaventure. *Bonaventure: The Soul's Journey to God, The Tree of Life, The Life of St. Francis.* New York: Paulist, 1978.
Buchanan, Mark. *Spiritual Rhythm: Being with Jesus Every Season of Your Soul.* Grand Rapids: Zondervan, 2010.

Bibliography

Cassian, John. *Conferences*. In vo. 11 of *Nicene and Post-Nicene Fathers*, ser. 2, edited by Philip Schaff and Henry Wace. Peabody, MA: Hendrickson, 1995.

Chadwick, Owen, editor. *Western Asceticism*. Philadelphia: Westminster, 1958.

Chan, Simon. *Spiritual Theology: A Systematic Study of the Christian Life*. Downers Grove, IL: InterVarsity, 1998.

Chase, Steven. *The Tree of Life: Models of Christian Prayer*. Grand Rapids: Baker, 2005.

Chittister, Joan. *Wisdom Distilled from the Daily: Living the Rule of St. Benedict Today*. San Francisco: HarperSanFrancisco, 1990.

De Waal, Esther. *Lost in Wonder: Rediscovering the Spiritual Art of Attentiveness*. Collegeville, MN: Liturgical, 2003.

Doughty, Stephen V. "Adrift." *Weavings* 16/2 (2001) 16–22.

Eckhart, Meister. "German Sermon 39." In *Meister Eckhart: Teacher and Preacher*, edited by Bernard McGinn. New York: Paulist, 1986.

Einstein, Albert. *Ideas and Opinions*. Translated by Sonja Bargmann. New York: Bonanza, 1988.

Foucauld, Charles de. *Charles de Foucauld: Writings*. Selected with an Introduction by Robert Ellsberg. New York: Orbis, 1999.

Gallagher, Winifred. *The Power of Place: How Our Surroundings Shape Our Thoughts, Emotions, and Actions*. New York: Harper Perennial, 2007.

Gorlick, Adam. "Is Crime a Virus or Beast"? *Sanford Report*, February 23, 2011. Online: http://news.stanford.edu/news/2011/february/metaphor-crime-study-022311.html.

Greary, James. *I Is an Other: The Secret Life of Metaphor and How It Shapes the Way We See the World*. New York: HarperCollins, 2011.

Griffeth, William, editor. *The Garden Book of Verse*. New York: Morrow, 1932.

Heschel, Abraham J. *Man Is Not Alone: A Philosophy of Religion*. New York: Farrar, Straus and Young, 1951.

Hiebert, Theodore. *Eden: Moral Power of a Biblical Landscape*. Waco, TX: Center for Christian Ethics at Baylor University, 2002. Online: http://www.baylor.edu/christianethics/Creationarticlehiebert.pdf.

Houston, James. *The Heart's Desire: A Guide to Personal Fulfillment*. Oxford: Lion, 1992.

Hughes, Selwyn. *7 Laws of Spiritual Success*. Farnham, Surrey: CWR, 2008.

John of the Cross. *The Collected Works of St. John of the Cross*. Translated by Kieran Kavanaugh and Otilio Rodriguez. New York: Doubleday, 1964.

Jones, Alan. *Soul Making: The Desert Way of Spirituality*. San Francisco: HarperSanFrancisco, 1989.

Juengst, Sara Covin. *Like a Garden: A Biblical Spirituality of Growth*. Louisville: John Knox, 1996.

Kang, Joshua Choonmin. *Deep-Rooted in Christ: The Way of Transformation*. Downers Grove, IL: InterVarsity, 2007.

Kahneman, Daniel. *Thinking, Fast and Slow*. London: Penguin, 2011.

Bibliography

Keating, Thomas. *The Human Condition: Contemplation and Transformation.* New York: Paulist, 1999.

———. *Open Mind, Open Heart: The Contemplation of the Gospel.* New York: Continuum, 2004.

Kelly, Thomas. *A Testament of Devotion.* San Francisco: HarperSanFrancisco, 1996.

Kidd, Sue Monk. *God's Joyful Surprise: Finding Yourself Loved.* San Francisco: Harper, 1987.

———. "Live Welcoming to All." *Weavings* 12/5 (1997) 9.

Krakauer, Jon. *Into Thin Air: A Personal Account of the Mount Everest Disaster.* New York: Doubleday, 1997.

Kurtz, Stephen A. "Silence." *Commonweal,* March 1984, 137.

Lane, Belden C. *Ravished by Beauty: The Surprising Legacy of Reformed Spirituality.* New York: Oxford University Press, 2011.

———. *The Solace of Fierce Landscapes: Exploring Desert and Mountain Spirituality.* Oxford: Oxford University Press, 1998.

LaNoue, Deirdre. *The Spiritual Legacy of Henri Nouwen.* New York: Continuum, 2000.

Lawrence, Brother. *The Practice of the Presence of God: The Best Rule of the Holy Life.* New York: Revell, 1895.

Leech, Kenneth. *Soul Friend: Spiritual Direction in the Modern World.* Harrisburg: Morehouse, 2001.

John, Climacus. *The Ladder of Divine Ascent.* Translation by Colm Luibheid and Norman Russell. Classics of Western Spirituality. New York: Paulist, 1982.

Lumby, Jacky, and Fenwick W. English. *Leadership as Lunacy,* ch. 1. Online: http://www.sagepub.com/upm-data/37973_chapter_1_The_Presence_and_Power_of_Metaphors.pdf.

Mah, Mark. *Being Truly Human: The Desert Way of Spiritual Formation.* Eugene, OR: Resource Publications, 2012.

McGrath, Alister E. *The Journey: A Pilgrim in the Lands of the Spirit.* London: Hodder & Stoughton, 1999.

Merton, Thomas. *New Seeds of Contemplation.* New York: New Directions, 1962.

Miller, Anne. *Metaphorically Selling: How to Use the Magic of Metaphors to Sell, Persuade, and Explain Anything to Anyone.* New York: Chiron, 2004.

Mitchell, Richard G. *Mountain Experience: The Psychology and Sociology of Adventure.* Chicago: University of Chicago Press, 1983.

Mogabgab John S. "Editor's Introduction." *Weavings* 16/2 (2001) 2–3.

———. "Editor's Introduction." *Weavings* 16/4 (2001) 2–3.

Moore, Thomas. *Care of the Soul: A Guide for Cultivating Depth and Sacredness in Everyday Live.* New York: HarperCollins, 1994.

Morris, Robert C. "Riding the Wild Mountain Ox." *Weavings* 16/4 (2001) 7–13.

Mulholland, M. Robert. *Invitation to a Journey: A Road Map for Spiritual Formation.* Downers Grove, IL: InterVarsity, 1993.

Bibliography

———. "Life in the Desert." *Weavings* 16/3 (2001) 21–28.
Norris, Kathleen. *Dakota: A Spiritual Geography.* New York: Ticknor & Fields, 1993.
Nouwen, Henri. *Clowning in Rome: Reflections on Solitude, Celibacy, Prayer and Contemplation.* Westminster, MD: Christian Classics, 1979.
———. *Creative Ministry.* New York: Doubleday Image, 1971
———. *Our Greatest Gift: A Meditation on Dying and Caring.* San Francisco: HarperSanFrancisco, 1994.
———. *Reaching Out: Three Movements of the Spiritual Life.* New York: Doubleday, 1975.
Palmer, Parker. *A Hidden Wholeness: The Journey Toward an Undivided Life.* San Francisco: Jossey-Bass, 2004.
Pascal, Blaise. *Pensees.* Translated by John Warrington. London: J. M. Dent, 1973.
Pennington, Basil. "Bernard's Challenge." *Weavings* 15/3 (2000) 21–23.
———. "Tabor: Icon of Contemplation." *Weavings* 16/4 (2001) 32–35.
Peterson, Eugene. *Answering God: The Psalms as Tools for Prayer.* New York: Harper Collins, 1989.
———. *Christ Plays in Ten Thousand Places: A Conversation in Spiritual Theology.* Grand Rapids: Eerdmans, 2005.
———. *Earth and Altar: The Community of Prayer in a Self-Bound Society.* Downers Grove, IL: InterVarsity, 1985.
———. *The Jesus Way: A Conversation on the Ways That Jesus Is the Way.* Grand Rapids: Eerdmans, 2007.
———. *The Message: The New Testament in Contemporary Language.* Colorado Springs: NavPress, 1993.
Pirsig, Robert. *Zen and the Art of Motorcycle Maintenance.* New York: W. Morrow, 1974.
Rensberger, David. "Deserted Spaces." *Weavings* 16/3 (2001) 6–13.
Robinson, Tim. *Setting Foot on the Shores of Connemara & Other Writings.* Dublin: Lilliput, 1996.
Scazzero, Peter. *Emotionally Healthy Spirituality: Unleash a Revolution in Your Life in Christ.* Nashville: T. Nelson, 2006.
Scott, Peck M. *The Road Less Travelled.* London: Arrow, 1990.
Seitz, Ron. *Song for Nobody: A Memory Vision of Thomas Merton.* Ligouri, MI: Triumph, 1993.
Shaw, Luci. "The Need to Pay Attention." *Weavings* 16/4 (2001) 16–23.
Silf, Margaret. *Landscapes of Prayer: Finding God in Your World and Your Life.* Oxford: Lion, 2011.
Sittser, Gerald. *Water from a Deep Well: Christian Spirituality from Early Martyrs to Modern Missionaries.* Downers Grove, IL: InterVarsity, 2007.
Thompson, Majorie. *Soul Feast: An Invitation to the Christian Spiritual Life.* Louisville: Westminster John Knox, 1995.
Thurston Bonnie B. *The Spiritual Landscape of Mark.* Collegeville, MN: Liturgical, 2008.

Bibliography

Tuan, Yi-Fu. *Space and Place: The Perspective of Experience*. Minneapolis: University of Minnesota Press, 2011.

Vanier, Jean. *Becoming Human*. Toronto: Anansi, 1998.

Waddel, Helen, translator. *The Desert Fathers: Translations from the Latin*. New York: Vintage, 1998.

Ward, Benedicta, translator. *The Sayings of the Desert Fathers: The Alphabetical Collection*. Cistercian Studies Series 59. Kalamazo, MI: Cistercian, 1975.

Weil, Simone. *The Need for Roots: Prelude to a Declaration of Duties toward Mankind*. Translated by Arthur Willis. New York: Harper Colophon, 1971.

Williams, Michael E. "Gentle and Humble of Heart—Humility as a Response to Imperial Christianity." *Weavings* 15/3 (2000) 10–13.

Yancey, Philip. *Prayer: Does It Make Any Difference?* London: Hodder & Stoughton, 2008.

Zalensky, Elizabeth, and Gilbert, Lela. *Windows to Heaven: Introducing Icons to Protestants and Catholics*. Grand Rapids: Brazos, 2005.

www.ingramcontent.com/pod-product-compliance
Lightning Source LLC
Chambersburg PA
CBHW070501090426
42735CB00012B/2641